Sharan-Jeet Shan

In My Own Name

An Autobiography

Series editor: Judith Baxter

The right of the
University of Cambridge
to print and sell
all manner of books
was granted by
Henry VIII in 1534.
The University has printed
and published continuously
since 1584.

CAMBRIDGE UNIVERSITY PRESS

Cambridge   New York   Port Chester
Melbourne   Sydney

Published by the Press Syndicate of the University of Cambridge
The Pitt Building, Trumpington Street, Cambridge CB2 1RP
40 West 20th Street, New York, NY 10011, USA
10 Stamford Road, Oakleigh, Melbourne 3166, Australia

First published 1985 by The Women's Press Ltd
First published in this edition by Cambridge University Press 1990

Printed in Great Britain by Redwood Press Limited, Melksham, Wiltshire

British Library Cataloguing in Publication Data
Shan, Sharan-Jeet, 1945–
In my own name: an autobiography—
(Wildfire books).
1. Great Britain. Sikh women. Social life.
I. Title
941.0858082

ISBN 0 521 38558 X

GO

To
Khushwant and Arune-Preet
For giving a measure of peace and reality to my existence

To
Aziz Mohammed
For all the love that was left
unsaid and unexpressed

Author's introduction

Sharan-Jeet Shan was born in the Punjab in India in 1945, and came to Britain in 1966. She lives in Birmingham with her two sons where, until recently, she taught mathematics and worked as a youth leader in her spare time. She is now a science advisory teacher for Birmingham Education Authority.

She feels a deep commitment to Ethnic Arts and minority languages, and does much to promote them. For some time she has given talks and seminars on issues of equality and justice. She is also one of a handful of teachers committed to writing anti-sexist curriculum materials in science and mathematics. Her next publication is Mathematics for Equality and Justice *from Trantam Books.*

I see my book as a very simple and honest account of how I raised myself out of a groove, in which every role I played had been defined by someone else. My story tells of how I cut the suffocating cord with my past and learnt to live with a certain degree of control over my life.

The inspiration for writing my autobiography came from a desire to sort out my confusion about my father. He gave me the tools for liberating myself and taught me to reason things out with infallible logic. Yet he turned against me when I applied his teachings to my own life. His anger towards me for falling in love with a man from another religion was understandable. But I wanted to know what gave him the right to control my life so completely that he could banish me to utter isolation.

My father was a highly intelligent and a very well-read man. He inspired me to study as much as I wanted to. He engaged me in a critical dialogue about any opinions I came to form. By his rules I developed a hunger for learning and an ability to base my opinions on hard evidence. I was given Nehru's and Gandhi's books to read as a child. In addition, I had to memorise and understand the meaning of Guru Nanak's teachings. My observation of the practice of these teachings revealed that, by and large, society did not follow what the great leaders recommended. The treatment of women was based on the principle of men's control over them, often in direct contradiction to the teachings. From this I developed a very strong aversion to the notion of women being born and brought up in a mould set by society. Even today, this mould restricts either their career, and/or their choice of partner, as in my case. Guru Nanak's teachings placed a strong emphasis on both men and women taking control of their own actions and, hence, their destiny. For me, this meant asserting my rights as a human being and valuing myself.

Once I had decided that writing was the best way to heal myself, it became an obsession. I mostly wrote at night because, during the day, I was at work. It took six months to finish the first draft of the manuscript. I did not find it difficult to recall the past. We often remember the best and the worst. My childhood and youth stand out in my memory as a mixture of the most enthralling kind of existence and the worst kind of gloom. The memories are still very vivid and detailed in my head.

School was from 7 am to 1 pm. For the other half of the day, I helped my mother in the household chores, flew kites, travelled on local steam trains, and looked after my younger sisters. We had no television or toys. We climbed trees, played Monopoly, Ludo, khoh, rope skipping and marbles. Free India was very young and while at college, political debate and discussion were high on the agenda. Sometimes, I feel very sad for my sons as well as my pupils. Despite some of the best toys and leisure amenities at their disposal, they do not have the chance to enjoy outdoors as much, or the opportunity to create their own entertainment. It seems to me that teenagers are rarely interested in politics.

The gloom has overshadowed my life for ever. Separation from my family meant having to bring up my children without their support and love. Making my own life in a society which brands me as second class at both a personal and professional level has meant a continuous struggle. I have great difficulty in understanding why families wish to be nuclear. Surely lots of loving connections like the ones you find in extended families give children a better chance of feeling secure and loved?

The book was not written with a particular reader in mind. I wanted to reach out to Asian women so that I could make some connection with women of my own generation. When the book was published, I was very surprised to receive hundreds of letters from young Asians, both men and women, some in their late teens. A wave of letters came from non-Asian women from all over the world, who had felt their own restricted role as housewives and mothers reflected in mine. Two letters which had the most impact on me were from two convicted men in prison. They had tried to defend their daughters from domestic violence and had taken the law into their own hands.

Exposure to the media and constant questioning by a very attentive audience wherever I went helped me to decide what to do with my hard earned freedom. Whoever read my book was provoked to make some strong comment on it. This forced me to consider the impact the book had on its readers, particularly young people. I was amazed to discover how many got angry on my behalf. I realised that, even though I had written a very personal story, I had, by a quirk of fate, the privilege to be in contact with young people, both black and white. I value this above all other achievements and now my writing is directed towards one aim – to encourage a critical debate about our responsibilities towards young people.

I am always ready to answer my critics, some of whom objected to the book on the grounds that it may be used to stereotype Asian men. I believe I can easily answer these critics. They are like my father – one set of rules for themselves and another for the masses. People who criticise my book have not known the kind of oppression that I am writing about. They are often free to decide the course of their own life. If they want to make value judgements, they should read my book again. They should try to understand that above all else it is my culture, my history and my religion which continue to give me the strength to raise my voice against oppression. I would like young people reading my book to get a complete picture. No culture is wholly good or bad. Extreme cases of child abuse in England do not mean that child abuse is part of that country's tradition. Any abuse is a form of oppression and should be treated as such, not used to establish stereotypes.

I believe that everyone should be free to tell a personal story if they choose to. I realise that my book may not explore racist oppression enough but it was not intended to be a work of fiction or an academic study. I knew that I had to liberate myself from personal oppression first before I could start to criticise larger institutions.

Now my attention has turned to the media and to our system of education which have, by far, the biggest opportunity to help young people to understand the structures of our society and its values. Often, these two systems support and create sexist and racist 'realities' for the young. Sadly, many young people and their teachers seem to accept these values uncritically. As an educationist, I aim to encourage young people to speak openly about their experiences. I also aim to show that the media and the education system have the biggest responsibility and therefore the highest level of control over young people. For, it is my opinion that there are no areas of the school curriculum which are exempt from the responsibility of promoting and creating equality and justice for our young people.

1

The Beginning of the End

It happened soon after my divorce.

Monday 10 October 1983 seemed to begin like any other day until Mr Clarke, head of the Maths/Science Faculty, caught my eye at the other end of a corridor bustling with kids going into their lessons. He wanted to see me immediately in his office.

'Oh dear! What have I done now?' I remember remarking with relish. The mists were beginning to lift and I was gradually learning to view the past with cynical objectivity. But Mr Clarke did not smile back in response. When we reached his office and he asked me to sit down, I half-guessed the truth.

'The Churchill Hospital have been on the phone, Sharan-Jeet. When he was last conscious, your ex-husband asked to see you and the boys. They say that he may not last through the night.'

'No, please Roger! Don't say that! It can't be—he can't die! I don't want him to die.' A hundred hammers were hitting my head.

'They have asked you to contact them on this extension. If he comes round, he would like to see the boys.'

He handed me a piece of paper and told the switchboard operator to get the hospital for me. The doctor explained the urgency of the situation. I telephoned Arune's school and asked the headmistress to tell my younger son to wait for me at the gate. I had called for a taxi; I was going to pick Arune up first and then Khushwant, my older son, from the training centre at Bradville.

The headmistress was waiting at the school door with Mrs Farid.

'You are not going to Oxford by yourself?' asked Mrs Farid.

'I'll be all right, really I will,' I protested.

'No, you won't and well you know it.'

'I can't ask you to take me all the way to Oxford.' Choking with emotion, words were not coming easily to me at that point.

'You haven't asked us.' Mrs Farid, my son's teacher, dismissed my protests and asked me to get into her car with Arune, while she apologised to the taxi driver for the inconvenience. We picked Khush up on the way and headed for Oxford. It was not unexpected, yet I felt quite numb. The closest that I had ever come to the dark ravine of death was 25 years ago when my grandmother had died at the hospital attached to the college where I was a medical student. Then, I was a teenager, surrounded by the comforting presence of my parents, brother and sisters, aunts and uncles. Poor Arune! He had only just come to terms with seeing his Daddy once a fortnight only. Now he was being told that he might never see him again. Khushwant's immediate concern was for me and Arune. If he was shaking inside, he didn't let me see it. At the Churchill Hospital, the doctor explained that over two months ago, a canula had been made in Darshan's jugular vein as veins elsewhere had become thrombosed. 'The prognosis for a diabetic patient suffering from chronic renal failure is a very poor one. Unfortunately Mr Jabble was not able to observe the strict dietary and fluid restrictions, as directed by the haemodialysis team. Believe me, Mrs Jabble, we did all that we could.'

Chronic renal failure is the failure of the kidneys to perform the function of selective absorption and excretion of minerals. When this happens, a kidney machine is used to clean the blood on a regular basis, so that the patient can live a reasonably normal life. The connection (canula) between the machine and the patient is made in one of the major veins, on the wrist. The doctor then went on to explain the reasons for the canula in Darshan's jugular vein. Due to the malfunctioning of the kidneys, and Darshan's inability to regulate his sugar and fluid intake, the fine balance of various minerals had gone out of control. The veins in the arm and legs had become blocked by the clotting of the blood. In order to carry on the dialysis, they had to make the connection in the jugular vein in the neck, but within days, the canula had become infected. The infection had spread to the rest of the body, which was now poisoned beyond recovery. The septicaemia had also caused blindness. Darshan had screamed and hit his head several times in extreme pain and agony. As the doctors were unable to do any more to relieve his suffering, they had put Darshan under sedation. Without the dialysis, he was not expected to last for more than a few hours.

We went into the private room where Darshan was being kept under strict observation. He looked so frail, deep in sedation, oblivious to the world. In his last state of consciousness, he had asked for me, for the first time in many years. In his last hours, he had needed me, all pride gone from his broken spirit. His relatives had not been to see him for at least five months. The social worker and the doctor said that I must find his brother's address and inform the family.

I telephoned Darshan's brother and sister-in-law and asked them to come and help perform the last rites.

'Our car has broken down. We are a bit busy ourselves with various problems. But we'll see what we can do,' was their curt, almost unbelievable reply. The boys and I stayed by Darshan's bedside for a while. I tried hard but could not bring myself to touch him. I froze with guilt and hatred for myself. I felt cold with fear. Arune-Preet called him ever so softly. 'Hello, Daddy! It's Arune. I have come to see you.' He tried to get some response by gently squeezing Darshan's hands, a calm look of desperate hope in his eyes. He looked at me and I looked away. What could I say to Arune now? Suddenly I felt angry at Darshan. So he had finally decided to walk away for ever, leave it to me to bring up our sons, alone in an alien land! I felt pity for myself.

The nurses on duty were so kind. They made us some tea and some sandwiches. 'If only I had stayed with him another six months!' Pangs of guilt gripped me. Both the social worker and Julie Farid were cross, but in a kind way.

'If you are going to start blaming yourself, then you are being very foolish. No one can live another's life for them. You heard what the doctor said about the prognosis.'

Yes, I had heard the doctor. It all sounded, well, so logical. But that was my husband lying in there. I had always known that he would be useless at looking after himself. He was about to die. Death is so final: there would be no hope any more.

There was no change in him during the next three days and, on the morning of 13 October he died. Letters of condolence came from everywhere. My father-in-law reassured us in his letters, written with a shaking hand and a broken heart. He wrote to the boys in English. It was a splendid gesture.

Veer Malkeet, my cousin, wrote a touching poem in his usual style, understanding the turmoil in my soul. My sister Inder-Jeet's tender message clearly reflected her tears of grief and rage for me. But there was no letter from my parents. They had always advocated themselves as *Gurmukh*, God-minded, god-like, like one who has conquered *haumai* (self-importance). And yet, they had found it impossible to be charitable, even towards their grandsons. They had proclaimed their judgement on me, well and truly. My brother Param-Jeet did write a letter: 'It is good that he died. He was no one to us now. It had to happen.' Embittered and enraged by nameless anger, I wrote back, 'How dare you make such callous remarks? Darshan was not just a 'no one'. He was the father of my children. He was the man I had cared for for 16 years.' Perhaps that was unfair to my brother. Not knowing any of the circumstances, he was glad that his sister was finally relieved of a life-long punishment. He could not be blamed for not realising that my infelicitous arranged marriage had been a curse, a condemnation for both Darshan and me.

I yearned and pined for a letter from my mother. I knelt and prayed before a holy portrait of Guru Nanak for hours 'Please make mother write to me. A few lines, just a few lines, if not to me, then to her grandchildren.' I begged for guidance. There was absolutely nothing to be gained by rejecting her grandchildren. Arune needed to be helped with this colossal grief. I was feeling so inadequate, so agitated, by his total lack of co-operation.

Letters came from my uncles in New Delhi, but that one message which I needed, which would have soothed, did not come. Was my very existence then a threat to my parent's *izzat* or family honour? Did they want me to die too? Or had I not understood this power of *izzat* at all? And what was left now, was there even more to pay, yet more punishment? What was to be achieved by this total rejection? There was no one to turn to now. I felt so alone.

How did I become an outcast? Why did my parents not support me in my hour of need? How did my father, whose pride and joy his bright young daughter used to be, come to close the doors of his heart and turn against her forever? How did it all begin?

2
Born to be *Parai*

The sky had the appearance of a beach that had just been washed by giant waves, as the sun retired over the horizon leaving behind a crimson glow. The rhythmic sound of the cow bells must have lulled the weary *kissan* (farmer) to sleep as he rode home in his bullock cart with his cattle following behind mindlessly. The birds seemed to be airborne all at once, breaking the silence of a warm autumn evening with their chorus of chirping and twittering. The evening meal done, the embers in the *choolah*, or primitive cooker, had been allowed to die down. *Charpais* (Indian beds) were being arranged in the yard as another day drew to a close.

'Go and fetch the midwife, Meeko!'

'Stir those embers and start the *choolah*, Nimmo!'

'Giyan . . . O Giyan, it's no time to sleep. Get the bedding ready. You are about to become a great-aunt.'

Maan Santo, whose commands like those of an army captain filled the air, was my mother's oldest aunt. In no time at all, she had got everyone briskly to their feet, and my aunts Meeko, Nimmo and Giyan had been spurred into action. The kerosene lamp was lit. Aunty Nimmo filled all the empty pots that she could find from the hand pump in the yard. Aunty Giyan, having made the bed ready for delivery about five times, paced to and fro, wondering if young Meeko had lost her way. Perhaps she should have gone to fetch the midwife herself.

Dai Razia, the midwife, arrived, gave a few short sharp commands and pushed everyone out of my mother's room except Maan Santo. Lots of pushes, carefully conducted slow and deep breathing, and everyone heaved a sigh of relief.

That was my beginning, a most uneventful happening. To Sardar

Ajeet Singh and Bibi Pritam Kaur, a daughter, born to be *parai* (someone else's property).

'What a pity! The first child should have been a boy,' remarked the Muslim midwife.

'*Yeh to devi aai hai, aisa socho*'. 'A little goddess has come to grace us. Why don't you think of it like that?' Maan Santo hushed her.

'Pretty too . . . Look at those big black eyes.' I had won my young aunt's heart straight away.

I was born on 19 September 1945 in the village of Dhootkalan, Punjab, India, at my maternal grandmother's house, the first child in a family of eleven aunts and four uncles. As the only baby in both of my parents' households, I received a lot of love in those early years. The first five years of my childhood were spent in Dhootkalan, my mother's village, and Mustfapur, my father's home town.

Though I cannot recall why, I always referred to my father as Babuji. Having recently completed a course in accountancy, he had secured for himself a good job in a neighbouring town. He was often away. As far as I recollect, he was the only educated man in Mustfapur at that time. Thus he had come to command a lot of respect from the villagers.

My Babuji had three brothers and two sisters. When I was born, the oldest brother and sister were already married. I grew up with and was very close to my uncles, Uncle Nirmal and Uncle Kundan, Babuji's two younger brothers. His younger sister, my aunt Kulmeet, showered all her affection on me too. I can vividly recall hundreds of happy hours spent with them. My aunt would take me to the village well to fetch water, and to collect mustard leaves to be made into *saag*, a kind of purée made with freshly churned butter, to eat with corn bread. I would travel in style on the shoulders of my uncles, as they went to work in the peanut fields. Just the thought of raw peanuts, eaten with fresh warm lumps of raw sugar, makes my mouth water even today. My uncles taught me to climb trees, play countless marble games and *guli-danda*, a popular game in the Punjab, played with a spindle-shaped billet, which must be struck with a stick over certain obstacles. At the end of a lazy day, they would give me a ride on the back of our buffalo, themselves walking on either side of me. At nightfall, safely tucked up between the two people I loved best in all the world, I would go to sleep.

The village of Mustfapur enjoyed the typical prosperity of the region. The Punjab is one of India's richest states and produces more than half of the nation's wheat and rice crops. By and large, the communities there are made up of Sikhs and Hindus. They have lived alongside each other and fought against the many invaders of India for centuries. Being a northern state, and relatively far away from the equator, the climate is less harsh than that of the south of India.

My brother Param-Jeet was born a year and a half after me. My mother and grandmother were always busy around him in ceaseless activity. For some peculiar reason he always seemed to need far more attention than me. (It was much later that I came to realise the importance of a son to Indian parents.) If ever there was anything to be shared, I was told to be a good sister and let him have his way, for I must have done good deeds in my previous life to be blessed with a brother, a belief I later found to be contradictory to the Sikh faith.

My mother, Bibi Pritam Kaur, was a very beautiful woman. The gods had adorned her with the most perfect of oriental features. Big, black, deep-set eyes, high cheekbones, and luscious dark hair were enhanced further by a pale golden complexion. Anyone could see why my father had married her. My grandmother insisted, though, that her son had agreed to this marriage purely as an act of kindness to my mother's parents who had such a heavy burden of six daughters.

I must have been about four when we moved to Karol Bagh in New Delhi. We had a second-floor flat in a relatively well-to-do part of the town, and were the envy of all our relatives. My Babuji had found a *pakki naukari*, a permanent job. This was talked about a lot in our village: no one from there had ever landed such a fine opportunity before. The job was that of accounts clerk at army headquarters. I cried a lot at having to part from my uncles, who were to join us only after their schooling had been completed.

It is with New Delhi that my most vivid recollections are associated. Mother's conflict about her lot in life as a woman came through transparently as she contradicted herself to me constantly. On the one hand she would outline a daughter's role as set out by time-honoured tradition. On the other, she would stop me in my tracks if my interest in cooking and sewing approached enthusiasm. 'What do you want with such skills? You should study and make something of yourself.'

7

She would often deliver this sermon to me, almost aggressively sometimes, sadness lurking in her eyes.

It was as if there was a constant struggle inside her. Though she never said so, it was clear that she had played a very submissive, subservient role, both in her father's and her husband's household. She would often talk about the importance of a woman being able to earn her own living. She believed firmly that lack of formal schooling was the chief cause of her own marital discord.

I would sit by her with my brother and study with indefatigable industriousness. She would patiently watch us while she was herself tediously creating the most breathtakingly beautiful embroidery with just a needle and some colourful silks. This must have been very relaxing for her, as I never saw her indulge in any other pastime. Everything in sight was embroidered. Borders of my *kameez* (tunic), my brother's *kurta* (shirt), tablecloths, duvets, pillowcases and even *dupattas* (long scarves) would be transformed from dreary plainness to works of art. Though she had had no formal schooling, she had incredible skill in matters of cooking and sewing.

My Babuji had the most vile and short temper I have ever known. Though he provided for mother reasonably well, he never displayed any affection for her openly. He would casually oppose and even rebuke her in public. My early memories of him are his earth-shaking explosions at the most ridiculous trivialities. He was a strict disciplinarian, carrying the concepts of truthfulness, honesty, diligence, politeness and other virtuous qualities to extremes. My brother Param-Jeet used to get involved in adolescent mischief: there was nothing abnormal about that. But if he ever got hurt, or injured someone else, it would have been unthinkable to tell my Babuji the truth. No matter what the situation, he would have laid the blame on Param-Jeet, and given him a beating. To save my brother and mother from his wrath, I would often lie. I was always punished. Violation of the moral virtues was never allowed.

And yet, I do remember the care Babuji would take. Before waking us up at half past five, he would have already said his prayers. I would stir from my deep morning sleep to the soft sound of mother praying as she prepared the *choolah*. Babuji, my brother and I would go for a run, and clean our teeth on the way with a neem twig. (The neem tree is known to have many medicinal qualities.) We would play a game of badminton at the Army Social Club. On our return, we would do the various household chores entrusted to us, while mother prepared parathas and yoghurt. By seven o'clock we would have bathed and breakfasted ready for school.

Laziness and boredom were unthinkable. 'People who get bored easily, are boring themselves. If you have nothing to do, you should spend the time in prayer and understanding of the holy Granth.' I am indebted to him for making self-discipline a part of my character. At the time, though, the military-style precision and the absolute obedience he demanded of me produced feelings of perfunctoriness.

One such experience stands out in my memory. Every evening, from the age of seven, it was my task to clean the floors, and search out the camp followers (insects), gunning down the poor defenceless mites with my aerosol spray. On occasions, my approach would disturb a whole household of accursed creatures. Throwing the spray high up in the air, I would make my retreat, only to find Babuji watching over me. 'Now then Jeet! You are not afraid of a poor little cockroach, are you?'

Though both my parents were keen for me to succeed in my studies, they also made sure that I learnt and did all the household chores. Two other areas in which Babuji enforced strict discipline were religion and literature. I felt no special calling to the holy scriptures, but literature: that was a different world. I learnt to disappear into the world of books, soaking up the magical, mysterious moments, some of which unfolded like gently opening flower buds, while others were like the stirring of a slumbering volcano. Even today, I relish the reading of a good book in preference to many other pastimes.

The world of religion, however, was very confusing. Up to the age of thirteen, I went to a single-sex Sikh School. I loved school and studying. But the contradiction between the theory and practice of religion sowed the seeds of rebelliousness in me. Sikhism had been conceived as the embodiment of the best of Islam and Hinduism, and equality and the brotherhood of man were preached most fervently. Yet my friends and playmates came under my father's scrutiny constantly. He would not let me eat or play with the children of our *mehry*, the woman who collected the rubbish and cleaned the toilets. Such jobs were confined to the lower caste (untouchables), the lowest order of human beings according to Hindu religion. Association with one's own kind was not just encouraged, it was imposed. I remember being beaten once by my mother with the *thapi*, used for beating clothes while washing, for bringing home a Muslim girlfriend from school and sharing my food with her.

The saying of prayers was observed strictly, *Japji Sahib* was said every morning after taking a bath. The evening meal was followed by recitation of *Rehras* and *Kirtan Sohila*. These were prayers from the Adi Granth, the most sacred holy book of the Sikhs.

Often, before going to school, I used to go to the Gurudwara (Sikh temple) with my father. He was the president of the Gurudwara Management Committee and their lead singer. On Guru Nanak's birthday, both mother and father would lead *Parbhat Pheri*, which is comparable to carol singing at Christmas, and takes place in the early hours of the morning. As the group proceeds towards the Gurudwara, more people join in while cups of tea and lots of lovely hot *parsad*, made from semolina and ghee, are offered from shops and houses around. To any child, this symbolic representation of the religion is far more fascinating and enjoyable than the actual preaching. I was no exception. In later years, when I had to delve deeper into the teachings of the Granth, I came to realise that in Sikhism there is an enormous emphasis placed on improvement of one's character while leading an ordinary human existence, and performing all the worldly duties. Unlike a Hindu, a Sikh is indeed prohibited from becoming *sadhu* (one who gives up all his worldly possessions). In a Sikh service, symbols and rituals have comparatively little significance.

At the age of twelve, I moved to a state school in Lajpat Nagar, New Delhi, as my father graduated to the position of superintendent at the army headquarters. At that school, I excelled in academic subjects. I was constantly pushed by Babuji in the direction of science and mathematics. I was very aware of and greatly disturbed by the deep hatred between Sikhs and Muslims. The end of the British Raj had left behind a divided India. Sikhs had always regarded the Punjab as their homeland, but a most sacred and strategic part of the homeland—Nankana Sahib, the birthplace of Guru Nanak—had become a part of Pakistan.

Although Sikhs were regarded as progressive and forward-looking, when it came to the role of a woman, the mixture of archaic traditions of Hinduism and Islam stepped in. As far as that goes, it will be a few hundred years before a woman's role, depicted as being equal in the Granth, is manifested in real life.

On the whole, Sikh women enjoy far more freedom than other Indian women and take part in most aspects of holy rituals and community activities, but various taboos, dictated by ancient traditions, remain. The veil, the *purdah* is practised rigidly. Virgin brides are still sought after. A widow's remarriage is not acceptable and a divorced woman is inauspicious, almost as bad as an untouchable.

One of the first taboos that I defied openly was the one on menstruation. Although it is a sign of fertility and femininity, a woman is considered 'dirty', physically and mentally, whilst menstruating. She is not allowed to touch the holy book lest she pollute the pure state of the menfolk. At the end of the period, a long bath and a special prayer allow her to be 'acceptable' again. I was so determined to challenge this farce when my first period occurred, that I forgot to learn how to contain the blood that would leave tell-tale marks everywhere. I was beaten by my mother who felt thoroughly embarrassed and ashamed of me and I had to surrender to the rigidity of this taboo and its related rituals.

There was no question of any open conflict between my father and myself. Children, be it girls or boys, simply do not argue with their parents. Opinions are only expressed when asked: forbidden to argue or state his point of view to Babuji, my brother would often take his suppressed aggression out on my mother and me. This led me to play the role of peacemaker between my mother and my brother. Disappointed by my brother's disobedience, she would often go into hysterical displays of weeping and wailing, a kind of emotional blackmail. Unable to confront Babuji and unable to meet my mother's expectations of 'an only son', Param-Jeet would turn to me for comfort. Both my mother and my father were distressed by his lack of academic brilliance. Unfortunately, the gods had bestowed those gifts on the wrong child.

For these reasons alone, the bond of affection and friendship between my brother and myself was unbreakable. The fact that he should always receive preferential treatment, especially from mother, was accepted as the norm by me. As I sit and recall the treasure of bittersweet memories of my childhood, there flash through my mind incidents which were to sow the seeds of resentment and distort and destroy the ideology of cherishing one's only brother. There were the special celebrations when my brother was old enough to wear a turban. He was always encouraged to play sport and take part in many extra-curricular activities, while I was confined, increasingly, to the four walls of the house. There was constant disapproval and criticism from my father, designed to suppress any 'fashion-conscious' feelings that I may have expressed. There were no such restrictions on my brother. Mother would secretly feed my brother on such scarce goodies as apples, almonds and vitamin-enriched milk drinks such as Horlicks and Ovaltine. It was considered vital 'brain food' for him as he had the most important task of carrying on the family name one day, and would be the provider in her old age. Not once was anything kept especially for me. If my brother was generous enough to share with me, he would get scolded, 'You mustn't spoil your sister. She is *parai*. She must learn to suppress such temptations.' Then she would praise him for being such a kind and loving brother, and burst into song. '*Bada ho ke, beta mera raja baneqa*', 'My son will grow up to be a king one day'.

It used to amuse me, this curious prediction. If all the sons of India were to take up the throne one day, what a glorious mess it would make. But, of course, this silly song was only an elaboration and illustration of the fundamental philosophy. According to my Babuji, God had meant us to have separate stations in life. It was simply *bure karam*, bad deeds in past lives, which caused one to be born a woman or to a schedule caste. If God had meant for me to enjoy the privileges of a man, he would have made me so.

There was a certain amount of rivalry between my uncles and my brother. This was created in the main by my father's separate set of rules for each. Towards his brothers, he would display ludicrous charity while inflicting preposterous beatings on his own son. I loved my brother deeply and felt very protective towards him. We were inseparable. Though it was not considered desirable that my brother should lend a hand in any of the domestic chores, he would often defy mother and help me with the washing at the community tap. This was the most tiresome and time-consuming affair as the water supply was turned on for very limited periods.

Brother Param-Jeet was the keeper of many of my secrets, just as I was of his. Two of my worst temptations were green, juicy, tamarind pods and steam railways. My brother and I used to walk the mile and a half to school, the Talkatora Road lined with huge tamarind trees. I would hoard, like a squirrel, pocketsful of this sharp, mouth-watering fruit. Mother would have killed me if she had found me out. We were both prohibited to savour this freely available legume, known to cause sore throats and give girls heavy periods.

For my crazy flirtation with steam trains, my brother and his friend Achal provided the perfect alibi. I would often take quick trips between neighbouring railway stations while mother took her midday nap, safely assuming that we three were playing Monopoly together. If mother was to wake up, they would make appropriate excuses and I would have to surrender all my pocket money to them in addition to doing all their school work.

My brother's attitude towards me was one of total reliance and singular dependence. There is nothing that I would not have done for my brother. I always felt very confused about my role as a daughter. On the one hand a daughter was referred to as *Devi* (Goddess), while on the other she was always being looked upon as a burden, a temporary guest, a duty to be discharged. It was almost as if the reference to *Devi* was made in order to cover up a kind of guilt a parent might feel for having given birth to daughters. Amongst people of all the three major religions that I knew within our acquaintance, a woman was greatly honoured as a mother of sons, especially by the in-laws, while a mother of daughters was ridiculed by relatives and friends alike. Exactly why the biological truth that it is the father who decides the sex of the offspring is ignored, I never understood. From the moment a daughter was born to the day she was married, one heard of nothing but the whole family's preparations and the sacrifices that would have to be made for the dowry to make a suitable match. As a result, a daughter invariably feels guilty for her very existence.

My mother had six sisters. As she was constantly reminded of this by my father and my grandmother, I used to be very protective of her. Until the day my brother Param-Jeet ran away from home, I had always felt a very warm and close relationship between my mother and myself. I would help her with all the chores around the house and she would consult me in almost everything she did. But Param-Jeet's running away from home altered this situation quite dramatically.

3

Param-Jeet Runs Away from Home

Param-Jeet did not have any special interests. My father had very special dreams for him as he was the only son and, regardless of his capabilities, he was expected to realise those dreams. When the time came, he was to sit the entrance examination for the National Defence Academy at Kharkwasla, Poona, pass it and train there as an army officer. To help him achieve this, I used to do a lot a research into the nature of the tests he was to sit. I had taken over that responsibility as Babuji was always busy with various duties at his office. Besides, he had no patience with Param-Jeet. If Param-Jeet did not grasp any academic fact, it was always put down to laziness and lack of effort rather than of ability. In my father's view, non-achievement had to be punished. After all, he himself had done brilliantly at school and college. And why should I have learnt everything with such ease and not Param-Jeet?

The only punishment, the only retributive measure he knew was the stick. Param-Jeet was fourteen now. Resentment about this physical punishment was building up inside him. He had talked often about running away to Bombay and becoming an actor. I had heard him and Achal (Param-Jeet's closest friend and our next door neighbour) talk about it seriously. They had told me of their plan and had made me take an oath that I would not tell their secret to anyone. I was to ask Babuji for some money to buy a couple of new books for English literature; I must convince him that if he wanted me to secure first place in that year's finals, studying the two books was absolutely imperative. Then I was to give that money to Param-Jeet. It was what my English friends would call Hobson's Choice. If I said no, Param-Jeet would get angry at me, threaten not to eat or generally tell lies about me to our mother, who would be after me with a stick. If I said yes, I would have to face the most awesome consequences. There was no escape from this emotional blackmail. How was I going to explain to my father yet again about losing money? I was getting desperately tired of explaining the fool-hardiness of his scheme to Param-Jeet. I wanted to run away with him to avoid the traumatic emotional drama that would follow in our household. And what about the effect such an impetuous action would have on our mother? I had read about the psychological effects of sudden shocks on people, particularly those with a predisposition to depression. What if Mother were to lose her mind or her speech or sustain some such permanent impediment? Param-Jeet was her only son. She already had very little standing in my father's family. If she were to lose Param-Jeet, her whole world would shatter. No, I could not let Param-Jeet run away. Besides, how would he protect himself against all those odds, natural and man-made? Bombay was one of the most corrupt cities in the world. I had heard of children being made into cripples and used for begging. I tried to argue, begged him to let me go with him, but to no avail. He kept defending his decision and told me that if I wanted to be a good, kind *didi* (older sister), I would let him go. He simply could not take Babuji's nagging and beating any more. He was going to run away, come what may.

The following day, I came home from school to find that Param-Jeet had gone. I tiptoed into my bedroom to find a note he was sup-posed to have left for Mother. There was no note, no letter. Mother had not realised that anything was wrong. I went on to the verandah. *Charpais* (Indian beds) were stacked neatly against the wall. I pulled one down and tried to go to sleep, but my heart-beat was so loud, it was almost deafening me. I could not sit still. I went into the kitchen to get some water. As usual, Mother was preparing the meal. She told me to get the plates ready and wait for Param-Jeet to come. She made some remark about him being late. I could not hide my anxiety and fear any more. Uncontrollable tears and sobs just burst from me. 'He has left home, Mother.' I tried to sound casual. 'He only wanted to teach Babuji a lesson. He will be back in a week or two, he promised.'

Mother looked at me. Her deep-set eyes seemed devoid of all life. Her lower lip started to tremble and she went as white as a sheet. I remember thinking, 'Oh God! She is going to faint. Maybe even die!' Instead, like lightning, her right hand fell across my face with all the force she could muster.

'Hold your tongue. Aren't you ashamed, talking about your brother like that?' Then, after a short restless pause she started shouting at me, tears streaming down her face, in uncontrollable hysterics. 'Why didn't you tell me if you knew? You wanted him to go. You wanted him to run away. You are his enemy. You have an only brother. A sister should cherish her only brother. Sisters all over the world do, but not you. Oh no!' And then she started hitting her head against the kitchen wall.

'You are *parai*. You are a *mehman* (guest). If he does not come back, I shall have no place to hide. *Hai Rab* (Oh God)! I want to die.'

I recalled that the mother of an only son is like a blind person; the only son is like the guiding stick. Without the son, she would have no cause left to live. 'Oh Mother, you have me. I love you and care for you too. I would never have run away and caused you such suffering,' I pleaded from a distance. I wanted to put my arms around her, to comfort her.

I pulled at her *kurta*, trying to stop her. She picked up the rolling pin and threw it at me. Then she sat down and started beating her chest and head with clenched fists, making a fearful sound all the time. I stood there crying, hoping for a miracle to occur, helpless, not knowing how to comfort my mother. I must have seemed like the devil incarnate to her. I wanted to go. I had barely reached the door when Mother got up, made a dash for my hair, dragged me back and started slapping me.

'You know where he has gone? Tell me then! Why don't you speak? Isn't there a tongue in your mouth?'

My tears and promises of truthfulness and honesty did not convince her.

Three days had passed since Param-Jeet had left home. The police had been informed. An appeal to come home had been put out in the national newspaper, the *Times of India*. Mother had not eaten much. Nanee-ma (Grandma) had helped me to look after the house and meals. There were relatives coming and going all the time. I wanted to help father by telling him about Param-Jeet's plan to go to Bombay but I dared not. Grandma was the only one who could understand my pain and my inner turmoil. She said that it was best not to say anything, otherwise they would only punish me more. I shall never forget the way all the uncles and aunts, relatives I did not even know existed, came and acquired a position of authority. None of them was concerned whether I had eaten or not, washed or not, changed or not.

Babuji did not exchange a single word with me. He had told Naneema that I was bad for the household, born at an evil moment, an ill omen. Whenever he passed by me, he looked at me ferociously. I sympathised with him. I prepared a cup of tea for him and sat by him, desperately wanting to initiate some conversation, to share his anguish. But it was no use. I kept thinking of Param-Jeet. Where was he? How was he? Had he eaten? What if he was already in the hands of pickpockets or thugs? A hundred worries leapt from all corners of my mind. Later, in bed, I closed my eyes as I pulled the white, cool, cotton sheet over my head to detach myself from this awful situation. I tried to pray. I prayed to Guru Nanak that if my brother came home safe and sound, I would fast for 40 days, pray for 40 days and make *parsad* worth at least ten rupees to take to the Gurudwara. 'Please Guru Nanak! Make my thoughts find my dear brother. He is a mere child. I don't want to live in this world a minute longer without him.' A future without him would be hideous. The present had already started to look so ugly.

Later that afternoon, Babuji came home with a Yogi. The Yogi had long orange robes, a white turban and a snowy white beard. I just stared. He was a stately, majestic figure. A look from mother was enough to prompt me to lay a *charpai* down and spread a clean *talai* (mattress) and a *dari* (rug) on the floor where Sant Ji (the Yogi) was going to put his bare feet. A clean jug of water was put under the *charpai* and Yogi Ji started to pray. After a short while, he asked for an article of clothing belonging to Param-Jeet. Mother brought out an old shirt and a pair of trousers. I gathered that it must have been to feel some sort of vibrations to connect his thoughts to Param-Jeet's. He prayed for what seemed like hours, then got up. By now all the relatives were sitting around in a semi-circle with their legs crossed and eyes closed. As Yogi Ji stood up, we all did too and he said *Ardas* (the Sikh prayer, equivalent to the Lord's Prayer).

Whether it was a miracle that Yogi Ji had managed to perform, or merely a coincidence, I never could resolve at the time, but next morning a letter came from Uncle Piara Singh who lived and worked in Bombay. He had found Param-Jeet standing on a side street near his home, selling pens. Param-Jeet was well and was being sent home in a day or two.

The following day he came home to a tumultuous welcome. Babuji sat on the balcony with his prayer book. He did not even lift his head to greet Param-Jeet. I could see Mother crying hysterically as she nearly squashed Param-Jeet in her embrace. All the relatives were taking him into their embrace in turn and gently scolding him.

As evening approached, they all left one by one. Aunty Kunti, Uncle Lashkar, and finally Grandma from the village. Babuji had to buy their bus and train tickets. I could see the anger in his eyes caused by all the inconvenience and extra expense that these relatives had incurred.

Later that evening, when Mother and Father had left to go to the Gurudwara to offer their grateful thanks in the evening prayers, Param-Jeet came and sat by me. 'I am sorry Didi! Truly I am, for what you were made to go through. I had to go though, didn't I? You do understand, don't you?'

Of course I did. Did I have a choice? I said nothing. He had come home and all was well. I was happy that no harm had come to my only brother. Mother was not angry with me any more. In time, they would all forget about the sordid drama.

A sadness weighed heavily on my mind at the realisation that I was not a permanent feature in my parents' lives, but a temporary one, a guest, a burden, a liability to be discharged one day like paying off a large bill. There was nothing I could have done to change this state of affairs, whatever my personal feelings. All their dreams, all their hopes of a comfortable old age were centred on their beloved son.

4

I Grow Up

I grew up in the India of post-independence, with a sharp awareness of social change. The English influence was a way of life, being absorbed naturally into my upbringing as were the combined elements of an orthodox home and a western-style education. My Babuji had gone up in the world. He was a superintendent at the army headquarters in New Delhi and, in this capacity as a gazetted officer, he held a strategic position of authority on the pyramid of bureaucracy. In India, most official documents and forms are acceptable only when witnessed and counter-signed by a gazetted officer. My father was the man in the middle, in charge of transfers of various personnel above and below him. At the same time, he had taken up a commission as a second lieutenant in the Territorial Army. His youngest brother, Uncle Kundan, had joined the junior ranks of the navy. My brother, too, had succeeded in securing admission to Kharkwasla, Poona, India's most prestigious army establishment, famous for producing officers of the highest calibre. In the highly-charged emotional atmosphere of young India, its army has always been accorded a very high position of authority. Mother talked incessantly about my brother and father being the 'defenders of India's frontiers'.

Babuji was proud of me in those days. I was always afraid of the puritanical principles by which he seemed to live his daily life. We lived in a big army house in Delhi Cantonment (the army district). These residential quarters had acres of land attached to them for cultivating. With the help of Beliram, my father's orderly, I grew all my favourite flowers and vegetables. Beliram was an elderly man who, though he was retired, lived with us in nearby quarters. He could never do enough for my father. He was a kind of shoe and kit cleaner, gardener and general handyman, all rolled into one. I remember Beliram as one of the few people upon whom my father bestowed his affection.

Towards my brother and me, Babuji showed no tenderness. I recall this with considerable pain. Even when I came top in class, won the highest awards for debates, I was not to receive a loving pat on the back or just a 'well done'. Poor *veer* (brother) Param-Jeet! He was constantly rebuked for his under-achievement in academic subjects. Life was to do with strength. To attain this strength one was to pray. And what if my fears of the unknown, unconquerable, cut through the shield of prayer and disturbed me? According to my Babuji, it was up to me to be pious, pure and firm against such a challenge. And yet he himself was not exactly above worldly temptations. Like all military officers in India, he always felt that bit superior to those outside his profession. He never let me forget that he was an officer, one of the ruling class. Therefore his *izzat* (honour) too, had a higher value than that of the *aam loag* (common people).

I grew up with Bapu Gandhi's pedantic philosophy on truth. I was passionately fond of reading those books of Gandhi which were about truth, non-violence and the role of women in Indian society. I can best illustrate this by quoting a few lines from his autobiography. 'Truth is not only truthfulness in word, but thought also. I worship God as Absolute Truth only. In pursuit of this Truth, the path is straight and narrow and sharp as the razor's edge.'

Kennedy and Pandit Nehru, the late prime minister, were our other favourite heroes at the time. Shelley, Keats, Omar Khayyam, Milton and Rabindranath Tagore's poetry were a constant source of inspiration to search for a purpose to one's existence. Like most teenagers of my time, I too developed a keen awareness of politics. Political fervour ran through all walks of life. We were the children of a very young India and were not allowed to forget the immeasurable price that had been paid for independence.

In the summer of 1956, a most pleasant change occurred in our household. My sister Inder-Jeet's arrival sent me floating on a high cloud of joy. A year later, when my youngest sister Karam-Jeet arrived, I simply went mad with happiness. I had always wanted a little sister, but two? What a bonus. Karam-Jeet was nicknamed Sweety for short. I can only vaguely remember Mother's discontentment over the birth of yet another daughter. But for me, those were the days of sheer enchantment. Their sweet smiles, chortling and chuckling filled my days with merriment and gaiety. I would look forward all day to going home from school. They would both be waiting eagerly on the doorstep. Every day I would take home a little bar of chocolate, running all the way, hoping to stop the chocolate from melting in the intense heat. They would eat, wash, change and sleep in my lap, listening to their favourite stories. As they grew older, Inder-Jeet developed a much stronger bond with me than Sweety. Sweety was Babuji's favourite, his baby. Being the older one of the two, Inder-Jeet used to give in to Sweety—always.

As the eldest sister, I was expected to set an example of the highest order in everything. I taught them both to read and write, to pray, to cook and to keep to a strict bedtime and waking-up routine. Some of it was done willingly, the rest was followed for fear of Babuji.

My future career had been decided by my Babuji from the day I was born, I think. Every one of our family and friends knew that I was going to train as a doctor one day: there was no question of discussion on the subject. Fortunately, the mystique of the world of medicine had a captive audience in me. There was only one other ambition I had, to become a reporter and a newsreader on All India Radio. Though this pipe-dream never materialised, I did succeed in becoming my school's champion public speaker. As in most other activities, in preparing for debates, standards were set by my Babuji. But my father's obsessive encouragement to rise to all of life's challenges also awakened me to question contemporary issues. Poor Babuji! Perhaps it never occurred to him that he was giving me the tools to rebel against the feudal, rigid extended family system and its caste-ridden framework.

The story of India's struggle for freedom cites unparalleled examples of the most formidable women. Nowhere in the world would one find such extremes of contradiction in a woman's role. In the struggle for independence, women had been at the forefront alongside men. Both Mahatma Gandhi and Pandit Jawaharlal Nehru recognised these deep divisions and saw justice in women's aspirations to be treated as individuals. The fact that, by and large, these aspirations have not become reality demonstrates our reluctance to change. The majority of women give in rather than rebel against parental pressure to conform. Those who rebel meet with such firm and fierce opposition that they often give up for fear of being branded an outcast.

From very early on, I knew that I was being educated first and foremost to enable me to find a good husband. Good here has nothing whatsoever to do with compatibility, other than social and educational. To find a professional husband for an uneducated girl, parents would have to be prepared to pay an expensive dowry. Higher education was an attractive alternative to upgrade a girl's value on the marriage market. Some social scientists have described dowry as a father's gift to his daughter to increase her prestige. In practice, it was and still is the cause of death and destruction, the heartless burning of many a young woman, the kind of cruelty suffered only by slaves.

The moral virtues that were imposed on me were precise. The scriptures, the cinema, and the roles demonstrated by one's mother and grandmother spelt out clearly the selfless qualities of a woman. Anecdotes, phrases and stories with a moral ending were used regularly by my grandmother to illustrate the womanly virtues. There was to be no deviation from those undisputed codes of behaviour. Most of these behavioural practices demanded far more of a woman than a man. 'A lady should only chuckle very quietly, never ever laugh loudly or talk too much, in the company of men.' I took all this in, and even today, it takes a very conscious effort on my part to accept and enjoy the company of a male friend. All too often, I suppress myself automatically, afraid to risk even a smile, just to be sociable. Coupled with the fact that the subtlety of English humour is not always apparent to me, I rise to the bait of some of my acquaintances much too frequently. There are those who are kind enough to rescue me from my inhibitions by making it clear, 'Come on Sharan-Jeet! It's only a joke.' There are others who judge me unfairly as being inadequate, always appearing to be defensive, perhaps even aggressive. I tend to feel alienated in the company of men, taking them too seriously, not always being able to laugh at the ridiculous side of life.

Though my education was steeped in western philosophy, none of its attitudes were allowed to be emulated in our everyday living. One very strict code of behaviour was the kind of extreme reverence accorded to elders in Indian society. It was unique. Neighbours were referred to as 'Aunty Ji' and 'Uncle Ji' even if it was a first meeting. One's peers were referred to as brothers and sisters, to avoid the possibility of sexual contact. In India, we have terms of endearment even for our political leaders: where else in the world would Mahatma Gandhi have become 'Bapu Ji' (father) and the prime minister 'Chacha Nehru' (paternal uncle)? Even the moon is referred to as 'Chanda Mama' (maternal uncle) by Indian women. To argue with elderly relatives was unheard of. In defending an individual's point of view, one risked a lot of displeasure. There was a standard answer if ever I tried to take a stand on issues concerning me directly—'*Ham jo bhi karengay, tumharey bhale ke liye?*', 'Whatever we do, it will be for your good'. It was 'bad manners' to argue with one's elders. In matters of personal concern, my father decided and I obeyed. A woman was to do her duty at all costs, never to take any step which would dishonour her father or her husband. There were no compromises to be made when family *izzat* was threatened. In no uncertain terms, my arguments were squashed by this one expression of my father's supreme authority.

During the traumatic formative years of my adolescence, I was made to observe subtle forms of *purdah* (concealment). Though *purdah* was not as extreme in form for Sikhs as it is amongst Muslim women, there were many related practices in our Sikh household. Naturally protruding breasts were concealed by draping the *dupatta*, a long scarf, around one's shoulders. The *shalwaar-kameez* (tunic and trousers) was worn loose, so that the rounded hips would not invite glances from wandering eyes. I was discouraged from sitting next to my brother, male cousins and uncles lest I were to arouse 'bad thoughts'. Then there was the ambiguous restriction of avoiding eye contact with the male members of one's family. Shopping trips and evening walks were only permitted if accompanied by elderly relatives. For a girl to possess a sense of humour would have been disastrous.

It was during the gruelling, irksome days of youth that I became rebellious against the double standard of morals, especially in my father. Under the safe umbrella of marriage and cover of darkness I knew him to have committed flagrant acts of adultery. He would give me money to go and buy sweets while he satisfied his hefty sexual appetite with a sister of my mother. I vividly recall my first confrontation on the subject with my father. For some unknown reason, the sweet shop was closed and I had returned home within minutes. What I saw and heard made me feel quite sick. The door of the bathroom was open and Babuji was sitting naked on a chair. My aunt was leaning over him, only half-dressed, her arms twined around him. Mother was sitting on the floor in the kitchen, picking out little stones from the dal in preparation for cooking, and crying. I could not stand the loud, hearty rollicking sounds coming from the bathroom any more. As they heard me approach, my aunt quickly shut the door.

Later I told Babuji how repugnant I found what I had witnessed. Instead of showing any shame or remorse, he said that my aunt was only giving massage to his shoulder which he had hurt in a game of volleyball. I was sixteen years old at the time. When I questioned him further about mother's crying, he became angry and lectured me for making such an observation before giving me a violent beating. And mother, for whose defence I had risked my Babuji's disfavour, sided with him and joined in my beating. I felt shattered and let down by them both. I wanted to kill both Babuji and myself.

That was the beginning of the end of my relationship with my father. As I grew up, I came to understand and sympathise with my mother. A married woman must aspire to be a *pativarta istry* (one who worships her husband as God). In doing so she must observe *laaj* and *sharam* (chastity and honour). She must never raise her voice against her husband. His judgement in all decisions is superior. It is most commendable for a woman to control her temper as well as her passion, always remembering that *laaj* and *sharam* are the purest of virtues. Such an irreproachable wife secures a place in heaven for herself and her spouse. My mother may have accepted this hypocritical doctrine, but I never did become reconciled with any of it. It seemed very conveniently designed to conceal a multitude of sins on the part of the men only.

Despite bodily concealment and plain white clothes, it was my misfortune that somehow I would always be one of the most 'talked about' pupils. In public, Babuji would boast about my academic achievements and show off my prizes for debating competitions. In private, he would impose on me strict seclusion. The concept of *izzat* somehow applied only to me and not my brother. I was to exercise restraint and keep a healthy distance from any male associates. '*Baap ki izzat rakhna, beti ka sabse bara dharam hai*'—'To uphold her father's honour and family standing is a daughter's greatest religion.' Make-up was not allowed and clothes were of the simplest kind. No adornments were allowed except my mother's embroidery.

I had completed my Higher Secondary Certificate with flying

colours and was looking forward to joining pre-medical college. As the adolescent years began to shape my body into a woman's my father displayed a new kind of tension. The most obvious secondary sexual characteristics were a constant source of irritation to him. There was no question of asking either of my parents about the mysterious yet pleasurable developments in my body. In fact, the growing attractiveness of my physical features was now marked as 'evil' by both of them. As my brother grew up, he became totally misinformed and acquired a very distorted view of his own sexuality—sex was evil, unless it was practised within the confines of marriage. A girl had to be a virgin, otherwise there would be life-long trouble. 'A girl's honour (meaning virginity) is her adoration.'

Today, even in India, at least in the state schools of big cities, sex education has become a part of the curriculum. In my school days, one learnt about the facts of life very discreetly. A woman was the tool with which this 'evil' function had to be performed by man for the purpose of procreation. Advice on contraception and family planning was not available freely to married women, let alone to us; such issues were confined to the back streets. My grandmother always referred to sex as an 'evil fire'. There seemed to be a kind of guilt association with feelings of pleasure in one's own body, so any discussions on the subject were fraught with tension. As I was being prepared for a career that dealt directly with human bodies, though, I was fortunate to acquire at least correct factual knowledge of this 'sinful' activity.

While I would be given lectures on piety, my father himself carried on indulging in 'sin'. My parents were not suited to each other in any way. His angry dictatorial temperament was no complement for my mother's quiet calm and dignified manner. I was gradually becoming aware of his constant nagging and criticism of Mother. She had become very ill: several ovarian cysts, each the size of a tennis ball, had depleted her energy. Over a period of eighteen months, Mother had to undergo major surgery three times. Her illness had brought us very close. Household chores had become virtually my responsibility. She always expressed sympathy, but was physically unable to carry on. There were, of course, the usual *dhobi* (maid) for clothes and *mehry* to carry out the general cleaning. School work, alongside the responsibility for my brother and two younger sisters, imposed a rigid self-discipline on me.

Religion featured largely in my mother's life. It was her greatest source of comfort and her only means of social connection with other women. She spent a lot of time studying and preaching religion. Furthermore, she was the only person I knew who practised the key values of compassion and charity with zeal and enthusiasm. She was generous to a fault towards strangers and relatives alike, despite my father. One particular incident stands out in my memory. I remember how she once rescued a young widow named Kamla. Mother had found this wisp of a girl sitting on a roundabout, having been thrown out on the street by her in-laws. Her body half-exposed, she was trying to pass herself off as a prostitute. Kamla stayed in our household for many months as a servant/companion for mother until finally some man lured her away with better prospects.

Though I learnt to derive solace from religious teachings, I found most of the orthodox practices unintelligible. A particular one relating to horoscopes puzzled me most. Horoscopes were written at birth, supposedly by experienced astrologers. They were seldom true, yet their validity was accepted unquestioningly. As far as I remember, it was a trade handed down in families, rather than a product of formal learning. Horoscopes were consulted to find out the exact day and time most propitious for marriage, for changing accommodation, for starting new business ventures, even for boarding a plane and for travel to foreign lands. There is, of course, the universal belief in our destinies being shaped by the hour and star signs of our birth. An Indian would strive to match this in finicky detail, particularly when arranging a marriage. Engagements and arrangements are broken if, at a later stage, one's horoscope comes up with clashing factors.

For me, western-style education had brought about a realisation of 'here and now' which conflicted with Indian theories of *dharma*, *karma* and reincarnation. *Karma* is personal destiny as determined by *dharma* (practice of religion). *Nirvana* (salvation of the soul) can only be achieved by righteous *dharma* and *karma* on earth. Such theories were lost on me, and I was puzzled by the suffering I saw about me. All around, there were people, especially young children, being subjected to unnecessary suffering. Why did the 'love of mankind' not embrace them? Why were there millions of beggars, destined to live in nauseating squalor? I could not condone it as the will of God. My Babuji had no compassion for these ill-fated, wretched members of the human race. He was a self-made man and felt that poor people had only themselves to blame. While I would shudder inwardly at his attitude and total lack of sensitivity, he would warn me against the temptations of *maya* (greed for material things). Apparently, the masses of suffering, condemned humans were only paying for giving in to *maya* in their previous lives. And their *bure karam* (bad deeds in past lives) had trapped them also.

I could only see that type of religious doctrine as scandalous bigotry. And what about the burning of brides, the suffering of childless women, and the scheduled castes? Life for them seemed to be an endless punishment. Oh yes, we in India were changing, making progess too. Only we were not changing to suit our own social and educational needs. We were surging forward blindly to copy and emulate the materialistic tendencies of the west, leaving behind the major runners in the race—the poor, the illiterate and the ones who had not the good sense to be born into the right caste. We were eager to catch up with the west superficially. 'Freedom of thought and action' was an exclusive prerogative of the rich.

The day that I gained admission to medical college was celebrated by both my parents. Special prayers were said. Mother made my favourite sweets to distribute, and I was allowed to choose the recipients of the mouth-watering delicacies. I chose all the children I associated with, children of neighbours and servants alike. A giant marquee was erected, and all our friends and relatives gathered to congratulate me. I had not excelled at pre-medical college in quite the same way as I had done at school, and Babuji was disappointed over my results. But even he had rewarded me with a generous one hundred rupees to buy new material for clothes, and some books for college. I had lived up to my father's image of me, at least partially. I thought and lived every day for my medical studies. There was no time to be wasted. It was the noblest of all professions. I was keen and dedicated and totally uninterested in everything else: all other issues were simply mundane and routine. Once the everyday chores had been tackled, every spare moment belonged to studying. I was so busy and so happy.

For a while, the issue of marriage had faded from view. There was an unspoken agreement between my father and me that, so long as I was studying, there would be no pressure for marriage. He was going to look for a suitable match and, so long as I agreed to an engagement, he would not unsettle me half-way through my studies. There was to be no freedom in the choice of a marriage partner. I would, however, be allowed to say yes or no if I was not impressed at a carefully chaperoned meeting lasting a quarter of an hour or so. I was told that I should consider myself very lucky, as my father had his first glimpse of my mother through her semi-transparent *ghunghat* (veil) when he had sat next to her at the *lavan* (marriage ceremony). My father was aware of my strong views on arranged marriages and had promised me that he would take the utmost care in the selection of a spouse. I would have liked to have married a doctor serving in the army or navy. I trusted my father to be sensitive, at least in this.

I was never able to talk to either my mother or any other female associates about my greatest fear—fear of going to bed with a total stranger. Whenever I thought of the wedding night, the pleasant dreams of youth would turn into nightmares. A total stranger would come one day and demand to be the owner, partner perhaps, of my innermost thoughts. What if there was no emotional or sexual compatibility? My mother would have thought me mad for thinking such thoughts. But was it not our very own beloved prime minister Nehru who had said, 'Marriage should be based on a complete understanding, a perfect union of minds.'? How could that be achieved between two people who meet for the first time on their wedding night? On the other hand, if I was not to accept my father's choice, where would I meet the husband of my dreams? At the social occasions where a meeting might have been possible, such as religious and festive celebrations? One was always under the eagle eye of elderly relatives. There was total segregation at college. Although this had the undesirable effect of promoting a 'forbidden fruit' mentality, the final outcome was almost always unpleasant: escapes and marriages were often followed by suicides and passion killings. So why was I craving for such an unknown, unheard of concept? Social compatibility was seen as important, but love, as my father had advised me many times, had nothing whatsoever to do with marriage.

'You would grow to love one another.'

'But what if you don't?'

'Well, you'll just have to make the most of it, won't you?'

I wanted to tell my father that he had not grown to love my mother. But he would have disagreed. He provided for her and kept her. The fact that she was a mental and an emotional being too, besides being a physical one, would not have crossed his mind.

By and large, my father simply ignored my radical views. To me, an arranged marriage seemed nothing more than legalised prostitution. To my father, it was the most natural extension to one's family. If he was ever disturbed by my rebellious nature, he did not show it. It may never have occurred to him that I had acquired his stubborn character and would one day challenge the closeness and emotional security our extended family set-up was supposed to offer for, other than my two uncles, I saw the rest of the relatives more as interfering busy bodies than as trustworthy and reliable friends in need.

For a woman, every standard, every value, was the direct result of one tradition or another. Furthermore, a woman seemed to be like a standard-bearer sent out ahead, accountable for her every move to the men of her family. Her social standing was measured by this conventional yardstick. The higher the caste one belonged to, the stricter were the measures. My family were Sikhs. As the caste system was not practised among Sikhs, religious convictions superseded all else. A Sikh may only marry a Sikh; marriage to a Hindu or a Christian would be tolerated if need be, but *never* to a Muslim. This strong hatred goes back to the forced conversion of Hindus and Sikhs to Islam by the Mogul Emperor Aurengzeb during the later period of the emergence of the Sikh faith, in the seventeenth century.

No, I had to leave this most important decision of my life to my father. He had brought me up. He had spent hundreds of rupees on my education. Besides, there were millions of arranged marriages that were happy. And yet, as I looked in the mirror, searching the image, the mirror would seem to crack into fragments, reflecting not only myself but the sad, tear-strewn faces of my mother and my grandmother, who would simply say, '*Jo apni kismet*', 'Whatever the moving finger has written'. At least I would be independent economically. My father would choose a learned man for me. I would exercise self-restraint and never 'fall in love': that was a western concept. Meanwhile there was so much to look forward to. My medical studies would keep me happily occupied for at least six years, and I would not have time to concern myself with the subject of marriage.

I loved my mother dearly and respected my father for many hundreds of qualities, even though there were tensions between us. My first responsibility was to them. I was the oldest daughter and had to set a supreme example of self-discipline for my sisters and brother to follow. And yet, the pre-ordained unpardonable did happen. Those magical moments when Love laid the bewitching trap are lost now for ever in the endless tunnel of time. But the bouquet of memories with its sweet fragrance, fresh like the morning dew, excites my whole being even today, as if it were only yesterday.

Studies at the medical college were far more intensive than I had ever imagined. I enjoyed the challenge and looked forward to every new discovery about nature's most astonishing creation—the human being. It was about three months into the term, when I first met Aziz.

I was rushing up the stairs, late for my anatomy lecture, taking two steps at a time. Aziz must have been doing exactly the same, only in the opposite direction. I stopped and turned.

'Hey, Aziz, the lecture theatre is this way.'

'I know, but I am down to do histology practical,' he replied.

'No, you are not, you are on the same list as me.'

We walked up the stairs together, slowly. Something inside me had stirred. I felt uneasy, clumsy, and dropped my books. As he picked the books up one by one and handed them to me, I felt like running away. I resented the peculiar reaction in myself for which I could offer no logical or rational explanation. For the last two years I had been studying at a co-educational establishment, but no one had ever entered my private world in that way.

Over the next couple of months, I absorbed myself deep into my studies. Every week, we had a thorough oral examination on a specific part of the body that we had dissected. A doctor must be acquainted with the complete human system at all times. It was, therefore, of paramount importance that one scored high in the regular assessments. Latin names of every organ, and the relationship between the various tissues, had to be committed to memory.

My second encounter with Aziz was even less romantic than the first one. He had lost the key to his locker and had asked me for a hairpin to see if he could lever it open. Later, he came back to apologise for the state of the pin, bent crooked and quite useless for the purpose for which it was designed. We got talking and compared notes on various subjects. He was three years older than me. His school life had not been as successful as mine; he had persevered though, and had finally succeeded in gaining admission. From then on, we gradually drew closer, revising for examinations, borrowing each other's notes, helping each other with dissection and even competing in all sorts of ways in our studies. For both of us, gaining our medical degree was the most cherished objective.

Soon Aziz expressed his love for me quite openly. There was a need to be discreet to protect our privacy, but no need whatsoever to deny our feelings. We spent every spare moment together. We went for long walks in Buddha Jayanti Park and the Talkatora Gardens in Delhi, weaving hundreds of multi-coloured dreams together. Over a period of some twenty months, I truly grew to love Aziz. I knew that, for me, life without him would be incomplete.

Yet I was constantly fearful of the impending agitation that I knew our relationship would cause my parents; I felt I was cheating on them. Aziz had no such misgivings about his parents. He had introduced me to his mother, brother and sister quite definitely as the girl he loved and would marry one day. My acceptance in their household meant that there was a fair chance of success for our relationship. I spent many a happy hour in Aziz's home, blissfully content, well and truly lost to the world. But did I have enough grit to face my Babuji's ferocious temper? The very thought should have been enough to paralyse and freeze me in my tracks. Maybe, until the inevitable happens to us personally, we can only visualise it as something that happens to others. Our optimism hides the catastrophe from view.

It was not blind ignorance on my part, but hope and faith that made me approach my mother. She was bewildered at first by my naïvety, but later agreed to meet Aziz after the Gurudwara ceremony in the bazaar one Sunday. Mother liked Aziz instantly; his quiet, polite manner won her over. Although it was no use asking her to go to Babuji with any proposals, at that stage, her approval gave me courage to wait patiently for an opportune moment in the future.

Meanwhile, we progressed more than just satisfactorily in our studies and Aziz also taught me to read and write Urdu. To secure our position, we decided to put a recognised seal on our love. Soon after we sat the first M.B. examination, Aziz and I married in an Indian court of law. It was July 1965: I was nearly twenty, he was twenty-three. In a matter of months, I would have been twenty-one, the age

of consent. The plan was simple. We were both to complete our studies before Aziz had to confront my father. In the meantime, we would keep a low profile and meet only when and where it was safe. The day after we got married though, was 'our day'.

'Shanno! Are you happy? Look at us now. In the eyes of God, and in the eyes of law we are one. No one can part us.'

Lost in his embrace, I should have been ecstatic. Instead, an uneasiness filled me with an impending terror. The tentacles of tradition were closing in on us. I felt dizzy and suffocated.

'You won't ever leave me, Aziz, will you?'

'How could I? Silly, you are my wife now.' He pointed to a bundle in the corner and commanded, 'Go on, go change now.'

It was a most gorgeous wedding gift. A purple, silky *kurta*—pyjama outfit, which Aziz had had made, specially. There was a set of matching glass bangles and a pair of sandals. As I appeared from behind the curtains, he gave me a lingering, loving, possessive look, pulled me in front of the mirror and whispered, 'Look! My love has made you beautiful. *Meri rehna Shanno, sada meri rehna*', 'Stay mine, for ever.'

As a man, as a human being, he was simply beautiful. In our expression of love for each other, we were equally intense, passionate and sincere. Whatever the future held, our minds, bodies and souls had been enraptured by that glorious feeling called 'love'.

Over the next three years, we planned to do our best to achieve our ambition, learn more about each other and gently persuade our respective fathers to recognise our marriage. Without my father's approval and a religious ceremony, our court marriage would not even be considered valid. In India, no court would have challenged such an explosive issue, that of a marital alliance between a Sikh and a Muslim. The most important approval was yet to be granted, for in the eyes of 'tradition' my marriage did not yet exist.

5

Father Finds Out

When Subash, a militant classmate of mine, had first threatened to write a letter to my father, I dismissed it as a mere empty threat. Subash was very hot on left-wing politics and was always looking to stir up trouble.

'Why do you want to do such a thing? I haven't done you any harm.'

'You are stuck up. You think you are better than the rest of us. Otherwise why pick a Muslim?'

He gave me a lecture on piety and claimed that if Aziz and I did not stop meeting openly, there could be riots.

'You can't mean that. We don't live in the Middle Ages. Besides, it isn't any of your business. You are supposed to be training as a doctor, which is the most honourable of professions. You will be treating all kinds of people. You will take the Hippocratic Oath and treat all men as equal.'

'That may be, but we have to live in this society as social beings and obey the rules. And this society, our contemporary society, will never accept a marriage between a Sikh and a Muslim.'

Subash insisted that I break off my relationship with Aziz. Our argument became so heated that I got up to slap his face. He shouted some more of his dogma about Sikhs and Muslims being enemies and walked away.

I can only guess what he must have done after that. He must have written a letter to my father about Aziz and me, and offered to be an intermediary. In the following few days he avoided both Aziz and me. I had not taken his threats seriously. Now, I would have to pay the price.

The following day, Aziz and I were crossing the road together at

Delhi Gate when I saw my father in the distance. It was no good asking Aziz to let go of my hand as my father had already seen me. Besides, I felt a compulsion to tell my father about us. I was very frightened, scared out of my mind. He simply looked at me, his eyes like daggers, totally ignoring Aziz's presence. I followed him to where his motor bike was parked and we went home. I was told to go into my room whilst my father conferred with my mother as to what steps were to be taken now. Their honour was at stake. I wanted so much to tell him about my marriage, but did not have the courage.

That afternoon, with restless, fearful feelings, I tried to talk to them but they kept up a stony, heartless silence. The following day, father did not go to his office. He wrote hundreds of letters to all his relatives asking them to start looking for a suitable match for me straight away. He sent a photograph of me to each one. At breakfast, lunch and supper, my parents only talked to each other. By now a terrible fear had gripped me. Were they going to let me go back to college? Were they going to stop my studies and simply marry me off? But I was already married. No, it was my imagination running wild. Parents couldn't do that to their own child. I knew my father was angry. Once he had calmed down, he would talk to me. I would then put my point of view and we would take it from there. It was going to be the summer holiday period soon and there would be time enough to have a good argument and lots of talks. Surely he loved me enough to see my point of view.

Days passed, my parents exchanged no more than a few formal words with me. At last, one evening, I summoned up some courage and cornered Babuji. It was my future, my life they were planning to change. I could not let them do it without their even consulting me.

'What exactly are you doing? You must explain your plans to me.' I was shaking, trembling like a leaf, as I faced my father.

'We are looking for a suitable husband for you', he said, as a statement of fact.

'You can't mean that. I am half way through my career! How can you interrupt that with a marriage? And aren't you going to ask me what *I* feel about all this?' I could feel a strange strength sweep through me as I fired him with questions. 'What is a suitable husband? Why isn't Aziz a suitable husband? He loves me deeply. I love him too. We are both going to be doctors. Isn't that a good enough basis for marriage?' Just then, his hand struck my face and I remember screaming.

'Stop this nonsense talk immediately. I never want to hear his name mentioned in this house again. They are our enemies. Our Gurus sacrificed their lives because of these people and you are planning to marry one! We will do what is best for you. You have shamed us, shamed the Sikh religion, shamed all your elders.'

'I am nearly twenty years old, a grown woman. You...you can't simply end my career like this,' I said slowly, baffled by the half-understood truth of what he had said. 'Babuji! Please listen to me. I beg you. You don't know what you are saying. Are you telling me that I can't complete my studies?' I bent down and put my head on my father's feet. 'Please Babuji, don't stop my college. I don't want to get married. I want to study. I want to become a doctor.' My thoughts were spinning. What were they planning to do?

I wanted to tell my father of my court marriage to Aziz, but I could not. I was trying hard to figure out some step to take. Param-Jeet was at Kharkwasla, Poona, and was not due to come on furlough for some months. Should I write to him? No, like lightning, the episode of him running away flashed across my mind. I was labelled his enemy then. If he were to do anything drastic now like running away from the military academy to come to my assistance, there would be a permanent set-back in his career. No! I definitely could not have let Param-Jeet know.

If Muslims were so bad for Sikhs, why were the teachings of Muslim saints included in the holy book, the Granth? *Shabads*, hymns, proclaiming the unity of all mankind, were chanted with great fervour every day by my own Babuji at the Gurudwara. One of those *shabads*, translated, reads:

Allah, Khuda, Rab, God
Are all names for One
The world was born out of one light
All people are brothers in that.

The Sikh religion was said to have been born out of Hinduism and Islam: Sikh teachings contained the best of both. Sikh priests preached this as and when they could find an opportunity. They never failed to emphasise the greatness of Sikhism in embracing all kinds of people. I had always been very impressed with these claims and had used these points to impress my adjudicators during debating contests.

Guru Nanak himself was the only one whose life was an embodiment of the truth that he had declared to be the basic Sikh philosophy. One of his two disciples, who accompanied him on all his travels throughout his life, was Mardana, a Muslim who played the *mardang* (a basic stringed instrument) as an accompaniment to the singing of holy *shabads*. All his *shabads* emphasised this basic philosophy. Why, then, was it wrong to marry a Muslim? I loved Aziz and we had made marriage vows to each other. True, there had been no religious ceremony, but the sincerity of the two people involved was no less. So the biggest crime of my Aziz, my husband in the eyes of Indian law, was that he was born in a different religion to me. His other qualities, which would have made my life splendidly complete, were simply of no consideration to my father.

I felt angry and prepared myself for taking some sort of action. If my father was obstinate and stubborn, then I too, his daughter, could be the same. My father would have to accept my marriage to Aziz. Aziz was so loving, caring, considerate and always very definite and single-minded. What more could a girl have asked for in a husband? I used to admire his skill with a scalpel during our dissection lessons and knew he would make a fine doctor one day. As he had joined college about three years later than most of us, his attitude was more mature than ours. I always felt very proud that he should have chosen someone like me. I never felt that I had any special qualities, except that, once I had made the decision, it was him for me forever. I had been to his house many times and was accepted. He was teaching me Urdu and I was very keen to learn Arabic to be able to read the Qur'an, the Muslim holy book.

My parents kept up the silent front. Even Mother refused to appeal to Babuji on my behalf. There were few ways out. I could either commit suicide or run away.

Late one night, I heard my father shuffling through the letters he had received from various relatives with proposals of possible matches. Next morning, Mother had gone shopping with Inder and Sweety. I packed a few clothes in a little kit bag as hurriedly as possible, and caught a bus to the college hostel. Nina, my friend, had always promised to help. Now was the time to take her up on her offer. She met me at the bottom of the stairs.

We talked as we climbed the stairs and tried to work out some arrangements. Naturally, I did not want anyone to find me. We decided that I would go into hiding; she gave me a spare key and together we worked out a code about knocks on the door. I phoned Aziz and told him that I had left home for good and that I would now wait for whatever he was to decide for me. He had some relatives in a village in the north of Punjab. If I was going to be without a career, I'd rather hide somewhere until he was able to acknowledge our marriage openly. In another few months I would be twenty-one. That was the legal age in those days for a girl to be allowed to choose her own partner. I was perfectly willing to hide somewhere during those months.

Aziz and I had all kinds of signals to communicate with each other. He came the same evening. We held each other and simply cried. He didn't say so but, looking back now, I know how frightened he must have been. All I could see was that I loved him and would do anything to be with him. My mind was clear about that. I did not think for a minute that I could allow my whole life to be the business of my 'relatives'. Aziz wanted to protect me, look after me, yet he was afraid of the consequence of admitting such a union.

He came back as often as he could, reassuring me that he would find a way for us to stay together. I understand the behaviour and inward-looking tendencies of minority communities now, but didn't then, and therefore had no cause to doubt that he would find a way. I did not think then that there was no possibility of support in practical terms from the Muslim community. A situation like ours would be just the thing to spark off the hatred which was always there, just under the surface, amongst Sikhs and Muslims. I realise, now, the strain that Aziz must have kept from me when he came every day to bring me food and clothes.

Within a week, the college warden had found me out. She tried to convince me that absolutely nothing could be done and I should go home. She was sorry for me but, as affairs stood then between Sikhs and Muslims, it wasn't worth her while to interfere, especially as it was certain that my father would never change his mind.

Aziz and I together approached my uncle, who was then the manager of the Central News Agency of India, and he promised that he would help us to keep our affair out of the newspapers. He did not hold out any hope of being a go-between and talking to my father on the matter, though.

Within a couple of days, it was all over. The warden had managed to find my home address. Both my mother and my father came and took me home in a taxi. Like a dark demon, my father held out his hand with five sleeping pills in it and a glass of water in another. I had no choice but to take them. What strength were they? I had no idea. I remember vaguely being woken up and fed and washed and changed. My memory of those few days amounts only to sleeping a lot. I remember opening my eyes and staring at the lizards crouching around the walls. They frightened me. I thought they were coming towards me and were going to attack me. I could not have been fully in control of my senses: the lizards had never scared me before.

Mother came in and told me to get up and wash and change quickly in a very stern voice. Apparently, we were leaving New Delhi to go to my maternal aunt's home in the Punjab.

'What about college? Holidays are over. Please mother, look at me, I beg you not to stop my studies like this. I'll do what you say, but please let me finish my medical studies,' I pleaded.

'I am sorry Jeet, you will study now if your husband lets you. Whatever is in your destiny now will be before you soon. I can't change any of that.'

It was no use. It was mid-August when we arrived at the home of Maan Santo, my maternal aunt. She had been briefed thoroughly about the dishonour and degradation that I had brought to the family.

The effect of the sleeping pills had worn off. As I observed the beginnings of this fatal drama, I felt a new courage and strength surge within me. They were not going to break my spirit. I was not going to say yes to the marriage, no matter what. What was I expected to do? Erase the memory of the past two years completely, the memory indeed of all my childhood and teenage years, and fill that gap with what—a new career? A new husband? How? Why didn't they tell me how? And why were they always whispering? They were defining a new future for me, a future which was supposedly mine, but it took into consideration only their feelings, their age-old traditions, their gossip-mongers, while showing no concern for me, the person that I was. Everything was slipping away.

At Maan Santo's house in Dhoot Kalan, Punjab, India, I was made a prisoner from August 1965 until March 1966. I was locked up in a back room, with only a very small window for light, in the sort of room where grain is stored and the windows have metal bars to deter thieves. I was not allowed any of my favourite books, or a radio, or even a glimpse of the *Times of India*, of which I had been an avid reader. I remember how the most warm and pleasant moments I had previously spent with my father were often connected with the ritual reading of this newspaper in the mornings. We would race back home after our early morning jog to see who could get hold of the newspaper first. Sometimes, as we would come round the corner, the newspaper boy would see us and throw the rolled-up newspaper at us and whoever caught it could read it first. Babuji would often play a mean trick on me: if he happened to catch it first, he would take it into the bathroom and read it all while he had his hour-long soak. What had happened to my father, who himself had shown me the way of independent thinking, of being alert to my environment? Why was he discussing my future with other people and not me? He who had always taught me to be a private person, was now making my most important and most private affair public. There were no answers to my questions.

Maan Santo's house, which I had adored as a child, had become my prison. I was very confused. However, I was able to confide in one of my cousins, Bikram-Jeet, who was eleven years old. Too young to understand the drama, he was very willing to help because he had always looked up to me in the past as an older sister. He agreed to post my letters to Aziz and to bring me back the replies which came to his school's address. Aziz wrote that he would contact his uncle in the village of Tanda and that his uncle would come and negotiate. But how could that be? My father wouldn't let him set foot in the house. Aziz's letters were comforting for a while but, gradually, I was beginning to lose all faith.

Then it all started. One particular day, all the relatives had been sent away on some errand or another. Babuji and Maan Santo took me into the big store room at the back of the house and the door was closed.

'She has dishonoured me, disgraced me and disobeyed me. Ask her why?' Babuji was looking at Maan Santo. 'Ask her what I have not provided for her? Good clothes, all the books she has ever asked for, all the money she has ever needed.'

My father was getting very agitated. He picked up the *lathi*, the stick which was normally used for beating out the dust from the *dari* (carpet) from the corner, and began to beat me with it. I must have fallen and passed out. I only remember Maan Ji trying to stop my father as I cried out in pain and begged him to stop.

When I came to, Maan Ji was standing by my bedside. She had a prayer book open before her and she was crying. I tried to get up to fetch a drink of water. My head hurt and my throat felt extremely dry. An excruciating pain went through me when I tried to bend my knees or elbows, and I fell back, hitting my head on the edge of the bed. Maan Ji supported my back with a couple of pillows and fetched me some water from the hand pump in the yard.

'Jeet! Please stop being stubborn and say yes to your father.'

I put my hands, trembling, on her lips and said that even to think of any man other than Aziz as my husband, was for me blasphemous. I tried to explain to her that he would take me to his house as his lawfully wedded wife if father would let him.

'Maan Ji! You would like him. He is so clever and so handsome.'

'Are you a simpleton or a dupe?' Maan Ji scolded me. 'It can never be. A marriage between a Sikh and a Muslim—never! Besides, let's suppose for a minute that your father will consent, in what religion would you bring up your children?'

'Isn't a husband's religion, name, honour, a wife's too? That is the way I want it to be. Whatever religion he is, I am too. His faith, his values are mine too.'

I had no strength to argue any more. Maan Ji kept on trying to persuade me in her kind and gentle way. She knew that I was fighting a losing battle. She tried to impress upon me that the whole episode was God's will. There was good in it somewhere. How could I be reassured by what was sheer torture? Why would all-loving, all-embracing God want to separate me from my love for ever? Why would He want me to accept marriage with a total stranger?

I decided to defy all traditions and customs and go on saying no. I had never disobeyed my father before, but this was different. It was my whole future. After all, God could not belong to my father and his relatives alone. I closed my eyes tight and concentrated on the *Mool*

Mantara, a prayer from the Granth. I begged Guru Nanak to perform a miracle, to show me the way, or simply to take my life away quietly and swiftly. Like Maan Ji, I tried to find comfort and calmness in prayer. My elbows were bleeding and both knee joints were swollen.

Later that afternoon, when Maan Ji opened the door to give me a bed bath, I could smell the delicious smell of pakoras, a savoury Indian dish. As Maan Ji helped me to change into clean clothes, I asked her about the pakoras, and if I was to be allowed to have a few for supper. Maan Ji told me that they were making '*bhang pakoras*', *pakoras* made with finely chopped leaves of cannabis. I was quite alarmed. After the sleeping pills, what was my father going to give me now? He knew about my aversion to all artificial stimulants.

'Well, I don't feel very hungry. I think I will go to sleep now.'

'I am sorry Jeet! But you have to eat them. They have been especially made for you.'

Once again, my father stood by my bedside with a stern look in his eyes. Maan Ji helped me to sit up. My father told the old lady off for making a fuss over me. I kept saying that I had had enough, but he insisted that I finished all of them. My temperature had soared high by the evening. I must have been in a state of utter delirium. I can remember Maan Ji applying packs of cold tea towels and crying bitterly. Hallucinations were coming and going, and giant, twisted and deformed figures kept leaping at me from all corners of the room. I could hear Inder-Jeet, my younger sister, crying in the distance, screaming, 'Why don't you just kill Didi! Throw her in the well, or something.'

The inflammation of my limbs restricted my movements completely. It was all so hideous. My back was stiff. I couldn't turn over to either side, no matter how hard I clenched my teeth and tried. 'See! Guru Gobind Singh is punishing you for rejecting your religion,' my father was shouting again. 'Say yes to me! Ask for forgiveness and you can start your studies again once you are married. Nothing is lost yet.' Could he have caused any more crushing distress? How could he do this to me? Everything was lost. I was never going to finish my medical studies. Why was it so important that I should have said yes to marriage? If he was going to get me married, a yes or a no from me wasn't going to alter anything. Was it to relieve his own conscience so that in future he could hold me responsible for 'freely agreeing' to an arranged marriage?

Next day, my bed was moved up to the roof top next to Maan Ji's, at her request. Babuji was not afraid of me running away any more. With my badly bruised limbs, I wouldn't have got very far anyway. I wondered how Aziz was taking this separation. I looked at the clouds and the moon playing hide-and-seek. A tingling memory embraced my whole being. This was the same moon at which we had stared together, when Aziz had said 'Promise me just one thing, if ever we are separated, you'll look at the moon every evening at nine o'clock and pray that our love should stand the test of time.'

'And what if there's no moon?' I had teased him.

'Promise, Shanno, that you will think of me and these moments at nine o'clock anyway.' And he had held me tight; had been so possessive, so tender that I had wanted to melt my whole being into his.

The beatings went on day after day. The people in the village, who may have wanted to stop this drama, would not have dared to interfere. Educated people were looked upon with great awe and respect. They were feared like alien beings. My father was such a person, and quite a few of the inhabitants of the village owed him another debt: he had been a very useful contact in their search for jobs and a better living in the city. The migration of rural folk to urban areas in search of an illusion is identical in any part of the world. In helping the villagers to realise such a dream, my father had been resourceful. They were not going to challenge his actions and spoil their chances for the future. To have been to Delhi or Bombay, and to be able to speak a few words of English, elevated a person to the position of a Sahib. He was regarded as an aristocrat. Though why they wanted to exchange luscious green fields and vast open spaces for the dust-laden, smelly and narrow existence of a city, I never did understand. In the eyes of the villagers, my father was a man with superior knowledge. Therefore, he was not to be questioned. Beating a daughter in this manner beyond the limits of her tolerance was cruel, but what the daughter had done was shameful and deplorable above all.

Everything was silent once again. I must have been in a state of semi-consciousness. I heard Maan Ji's voice trembling, full of hysterical sobs every now and then. I dragged myself to the door and tried hard to listen. Maan Ji was talking to a neighbour.

'Both father and daughter are stubborn. You'd want to cry just looking at her. I don't understand his heartless indifference to her suffering.' Listening to their conversation, I felt very detached from the whole affair. My father was not a ruthless and indifferent person. Surely not. I had always shared all sorts of feelings about all sorts of things with him. I remembered gardening with him, playing badminton, going to prayers in the Gurudwara and visiting important people. I remembered how he used to get a special pass for us all to sit in the enclosure next to the President's on the Republic Day Celebrations.

I felt all mixed up. Surely it mattered to him that I should complete my medical studies? Why, he must remember the long hours I had spent studying for years prior to medical college. All that diligent study, hundreds of hours on dark, long, wintry nights; sultry summer nights under the street lights, with thousands of wasps buzzing around. I kept hoping that he would realise what it would do to me to lose the one career, the only career, I had ever wanted.

Nobody had decided his future for him. No dogma had cut short his career so drastically. Why did he want to destroy mine? I thought of a deal to make with my father. Though he may have been justified in considering my love for Aziz as wrongly placed loyalty, he must have understood my love of my career. I put forward the proposal that I would take a vow, by placing my hand on the holy Granth, never to see Aziz again, if my father would let me carry on with my medical career. I requested that he try me for just two years, even just one to begin with. I would go to a different medical college there in the Punjab; I would live with Maan Ji in the village and pay my way by working in the fields and teaching English to the villagers. By placing me in marriage with a total stranger, he would be doing the gravest injustice to both of us. I had already told him time and again that, in the eyes of the law and of God, there could never be another man for me. I was hopeful once again.

Maan Ji went to my father with this proposal. I waited in the back room for what seemed like hours. My heart was pounding away with this last little thread of hope. Surely, my father's love of tradition was not greater than his love for me.

The door opened slowly. Maan Santo's face looked dark and bleak, not at all like the bearer of good news. Even by the longest stretch of imagination, I could not have guessed what was to follow.

'Maan Ji! Tell me what did he say? Did he agree?'

She just looked at me in long silence. Brushing aside tears with her old wrinkled hand, she looked even more frail than usual in the dusky light of the summer sun.

'I am sorry! My darling Jeet! You are not going to be allowed to talk to me any more. He told me that the only reason I am encouraging you to stay here is because I want to turn you into a prostitute and thus have you as my support in my old age.'

My hands automatically clutched my ears. I went out screaming and yelling at him without caring for the consequences.

'Did you think for a moment even before uttering such abuse about your daughter? For the love of God, what are you being so cruel for? You are my father, not my enemy! You have locked me up, beaten me. What more are you going to do? Burn me then, or cut my throat or throw me in a well! Just get it done and over with. I will die before I say yes to an arranged marriage.'

He got up, I knew to hit me, and before I could run and hide in my room, he had got hold of my hair and pushed me inside. As the key turned in the lock he yelled, 'You will have nothing to do with this wretched old lady any more.'

'She is not wretched. You are!' I cried as I banged my head on the door.

'I shall make an example of you. Oh no! I won't kill you, or even cripple you, but punish you in such a way that no daughter would dare take such a step ever again.'

6

The End of a Dream

By February 1966 I had given up all hope. I had no physical or mental strength left to fight my father's continued beatings. I said yes to marriage to a man of his choice. Aziz too must have given up as there had been no letters from him for nearly three months.

The day Darshan came to see me as a possible match, Mother made my favourite dish, *makki ki roti or saag*, chapatis with mustard leaves made into a purée with home-made butter. I ate that mid-day meal to my heart's content and then changed into some clean clothes. Mother made sure that I was given a thorough bath from head to toe. After all, good presentation of even damaged goods can make them saleable.

Darshan's arrival caused a lot of stir. Fair skinned, of average height, but rather heavily built, he was a very handsome man. In his clean-cut English clothes, he looked every inch a foreigner. After dinner he requested a few minutes alone with me. Maan Ji, who had been sitting by me, went out with the excuse of putting away the tray of dishes.

While Maan Ji was out, Darshan asked me what I was doing in the village. I told him the truth as briefly as possible and said that I would try my best to make him a good wife provided that I was allowed to carry on with my medical career either there in the Punjab, or in England. He agreed and said that that would be fine. He had plenty of money and had absolutely no need for me to go to work. He was thirty years old and had been living in England for three years. He was the oldest of seven brothers and sisters. His father owned a sugar cane factory and he himself was a qualified accountant.

I told him that I did not need or want any fancy ornaments or clothes, only my books and the reassurance that my career could continue. He said that my simplicity and manner appealed to him. It

45

didn't seem like a good reason at all to me to marry someone. I certainly did not consider myself a very marketable product, even at the best of times, compared to what he could have found in the matrimonial columns of the *Times of India*. With all the excellent qualities that he possessed, why marry me? The matchmaker, one of Darshan's uncles who was also a twice-removed cousin of my mother, gave my father the details of the wealth of Darshan's family.

'He has a nine-thousand-pound house in England and a major share in an estate agent's firm in New Delhi. Your daughter will do well to accept this proposal.'

As I listened to all the comings and goings, preparations for the wedding, the ritual exchange of gifts, and women of the family jabbering away until late in the night, I felt very detached, simply an observer watching the beginnings of an unknown future. Everyone was simply dumbfounded by his charm, his sophisticated manner, his good looks and his kindness to me, who had absolutely no claim to any of these, who was dark skinned and had her stupid head buried in her books all day, who was positively plain by Indian standards of beauty.

I remember going for my first walk in all those seven months with my little sister, Inder-Jeet. The preparation for the wedding had excited her. She enjoyed the singing and dancing and such a fuss being made of her darling sister. She was eleven years younger than me, but often much more a friend than many of my own age. She was holding tightly on to my hand and chirping away like a parrot. I felt quite elated and light-headed. My thoughts were concentrated on one hope only: at least I should be able to finish my medical studies. I decided to specialise as a paediatrician. That would be splendid. I did enjoy the company of children. It would be a good life, a life worth living. My mind was filling with tentative dreams of a medical career once again. Our walk brought us to the *bhatti*, an open oven in the ground in which corn is roasted by the *bhatti walah*. I took out a bundle of carefully wrapped letters and Aziz's photograph and placed it in the fire. I cried in silence as the flames engulfed my love's last messages of hope to me.

I prayed that he should complete his medical studies one day and marry someone according to the customs of his faith. For me, the whole future rested on the ardent hope of becoming a doctor.

Darshan seemed a kind sort of man and I had struck a bargain with him. So long as he kept his side of it, I would mine. Tradition would allow this bigamous act to happen. It would be considered legal.

Inder-Jeet had gone to sleep on my lap. Suddenly I felt frightened and lost, just so lost. I wondered how and where Aziz was, how he was taking this separation. I remembered after our court marriage the way he had rested his head in my lap in Buddha Jayanti Park and had said, 'I would simply want to die if we are ever parted, if you are not there to share my life with me.' Words millions of lovers all over the world must have said to each other, millions of times. And now I was going to be made into someone else's wife. It was all wrong. There could not have been any purpose in it. Where could I go though? Nobody had prepared me for this new role. Questions arose again. How was I going to reconcile myself to this new situation? Why had my father not agreed to a compromise? Knowing all that he did, why was this stranger going to marry me?

'I can never love anyone else. My soul belongs to him. You must understand that,' I had said quietly.

'Don't worry! I have been though all these romantic notions myself when I was young. You will forget it all when we are married. You will like England,' Darshan had said, full of himself and his own dogma about life.

'Why should I like England? I like India. It's my country, my home, my land. I love living here.'

A formal death of my former self was about to happen.

The wedding ceremony was the usual pompous three-day show. On the morning of 14 March, I was seated in front of the Granth, at Darshan's side. All our relatives came in one by one, putting garlands round our necks. My sisters, Inder-Jeet and Sweety sat near me. Inder-Jeet kept looking at me, almost pleading for me not to do anything foolish any more. My eyes kept searching for Param-Jeet. Was he even informed of his sister's splendid 'funeral march'? I think not. I was told that he was not allowed any leave and that he would come to see me when I left for England.

Going round the holy book four times, I thought of nothing else but the hatred I now felt for my father. The last *shabad* that was sung at the end of the ceremony was ironic:

'Some call him Ram,
Some call him Khudah,
Some call him Jesus, and
Some call him Allah.'

But we are all one, we are all children of God. Were those words meant for chanting only? Were they actually meant to be followed, to be practised, to be manifested in one's living?

Everybody from the village seemed to have come to bid me farewell. More garlands this time, flowers and money. Relatives came in turn, crying and embracing. The girls from the village threw flowers at us, rose petals and snowy white petals of *kalian*, the plant that is called orange blossom.

As the petals fell on me like a shower of cool rain, I seemed to see Aziz standing under the gulmohar tree, waiting for me. My favourite tree was in full bloom. I crept up quietly and shook the branch just above his head. He turned round, covered in flaming orange and white petals. 'See! This is how they will shower you with flowers when you come as my bridegroom.'

'I shall insist on gulmohar flowers,' he had declared. There was a long silence as the moment froze for us. We both knew that there was no future for us in this country. This completeness that we felt in each other's company would shatter into innumerable pieces one day. 'And if I die from such happiness, please remember *nargis* flowers (small daffodils) for my grave.'

'Touch your grandmother's feet so that she can bless you.' My mother jolted me out of my dream. I did so mechanically. Grandma was crying. Why wasn't I crying? It was a disgrace, all daughters must cry when they leave a father's loving home. The garlands weighed heavy on my neck. I tried to adjust them to relieve the pressure. 'Let me hold some of them,' Darshan offered. He smiled as he took some of the garlands and put them on the back seat of the taxi. I tried to smile back. He must have thought that the sadness shadowing my face was just normal reaction to the situation. I certainly hoped so. He was the one person I could not allow to read my innermost thoughts.

Babuji came forward to embrace me. He gave me a hundred rupee note. I went quite rigid and said, 'God will never forgive you. I hope you burn in hell.'

His eyes burnt with anger. His hands trembled and I could see he was clenching his fists, wanting to strike me. I took the hundred rupee note, tore it in two and gave it back to him.

'Keep it Babuji, as my contribution towards the sale of my body.' He would not have dared to hit me then, in public. It had been declared by his law that I was now another man's property. Just then, my youngest sister Sweety came forward, crying bitterly, 'Why are you going Didi? I don't want you to go!' I gave her a hug and told her to ask Babuji. His last words about me will stay with me forever. '*Sweety Bete! Tumhari Didi gandi ho gyee thi, isliye hamne ghar se nikal di hai.*' 'Your sister had become dirty, so we had to throw her out.'

Sweety just kept crying, '*Didi gandi nahin hai*', 'My sister is not dirty.'

As Babuji moved away, Mother stepped forward. She knew how I felt. She had convinced me that Darshan would make a good husband and that my medical career wasn't in ruins. After all, he was marrying so late in life, he would naturally want his marriage to be a success. She was saying, 'Jeet! Look after yourself. Don't forget to pray daily.' I was not paying attention; my mind was still searching for a way out.

'Please mother! My darling sweet mother! I beg of you, please let me stay. I will serve you both all my life. Darshan will easily find another match.'

She must have felt so angry at having been embarrassed in this way in front of all her prestigious relatives, the relatives who had always hated her for her flawless beauty. Wherever Mother was, the hungry eyes of lusty men around her would follow her. She was richly endowed with the kind of beauty that needs no addition or subtraction. Her female relatives now had a weapon to get their own back; the disgrace and dishonour that I had brought upon the family would indeed make hot gossip. In their eyes I did not deserve to be so privileged. I was leaving India to go and live in England. They had paid thousands of rupees and worn out many pairs of shoes chasing entry permits into England. And here I was, an insignificant-looking girl, and it had happened to me automatically. Marriage to a suitably qualified and enigmatically charming man from England: what more could a girl ask for? Young girls from the village were watching from their roof tops, staring in amazement, full of envy for me, and perplexed by my lack of emotion. Little did they know that I would have gladly changed places with any one of them.

Uncle Nirmal beckoned me to go and sit in the taxi. Head bent, I followed Darshan into the back seat. As he sat next to me, I froze rigid as the most terrifying reality of his position flashed through my mind like lightning. In the eyes of tradition, he was now my husband. He now owned me and I was expected to obey and serve him. By Indian tradition, he was now second to God in my life. The dying voice inside me rose its head once again. 'Obey him, serve him, yes—but worship him as if he was my God? No! Never!'

As the taxi rushed past rows and rows of jumbled whitewashed houses, the village of Mustfapur was left behind. My past was left behind. I was beginning to feel tired and sleepy. I did not know what lay ahead in the future and it was no use contemplating the unknown. It was time now to put my dreams of life with Aziz at rest. I looked at Darshan. He had dozed off. Why was he sleeping at such a time? Why wasn't he showing some excitement as becomes a new husband? I felt very cold. An injustice had been done to him, yet he had known it all.

I had wanted to rebel, but now another thought was attacking every corner of my brain and making my whole being explode with pain. Had I really dishonoured my father, bringing his name down into the dust? Was he really never going to be able to hold his head high in society? I had heard of such incidents happening before. They didn't really make any difference to the lives of the parents and their relatives. Why then? Why was I beginning to feel sorry for my father? What were his reasons for not making a compromise? Was his ego hurt? Had he taken these steps to show his authority? Perhaps the words '*khandan ki izzat*' simply meant not to lose face in front of one's relatives.

In an arranged marriage, the first few days are spent fulfilling the rituals, exchanging visits with respective in-laws in order to get to know one's newly acquired family. During these visits, certain customary gifts are exchanged. A bride's prestige rests on the quality and the amount of gifts her father can provide. As the marriage had been arranged in such a hurry and Darshan had expressed his apparent dislike of the dowry system, my father had not provided a big dowry. Darshan's relatives told me that my father had failed miserably in not providing a decent dowry and not complying with the visiting arrangements.

At the end of the ceremonial three days, I was to stay at Darshan's house for a week, then go back to my parent's house for a week, after which a newly-married couple would normally have begun their own lives. Like everything else, the events of the following few days were far from normal.

In the morning, I was helped to wash and change into the best sari that my mother-in-law could find in my dowry. Then I was sat in the middle of the courtyard on a very low stool, a slight veil over my head, with all the dowry from my parents displayed around me. All morning, there was a continuous stream of women from the neighbourhood who came to give their verdict on the new bride. Some praised while others criticised and scrutinised my features, my dark skin, my clothes, my hair and, of course, various items of the dowry.

I had only heard of such customs with the village folk before, never experienced them. The humiliation of it all annoyed and frustrated me. The illusions of sophistication were beginning to be dispelled. Giddarbaha in Ferozpur, Punjab, was a very rural town. Its only claim to fame was that snuff was manufactured there and was exported to various parts of the world. It was a very neglected place with an old railway station and few shops. The only doctor had no professional medical qualifications, but was an experienced pharmacist who had declared himself a doctor, a fairly common practice in the villages of India in those days.

During the next few days at Giddarbaha, I came to realise that Darshan had been fostered by his paternal aunt when he was barely a year old. She was a rich widow with no children of her own. Her husband had been poisoned by his own brother as a result of a feud over the family property. The family included Darshan's mother, father, four brothers and two sisters. The younger sister, Santosh, had only been married recently. The elder sister was married to a lorry driver and lived some hundred miles away in a village called Lakhankalan. She had five daughters and a son.

My mother-in-law briefed me on the duties of the *bari bahu* (oldest daughter-in-law). It was to be my prime duty to foster good relations between various members of the family by making sure that the tradition of giving gifts on various festive occasions was kept up with the best we could afford. If somebody gave us a gift, we must always return the favour by giving a better one.

Bibijee (my mother-in-law) gave me a talk on the characteristics and qualities of a *pativarta istry* (one who worships her husband or *pati*). To begin with, I was never to call my husband by his first name. It amused me a little. What should I have done, whistled for him, or perhaps carried a flag with me permanently and waved it in front of him whenever I might need his assistance? My mother-in-law was not pleased by my childish remarks. She said that such behaviour did not become one in my position and that I must show respect and obedience at all times to my husband, as well as to the elders in the family. Though she was not happy that I did not veil my face, I must make sure that I never looked my father-in-law straight in the eyes. Indeed, I must draw at least half a veil when I saw him approaching.

As a *pativarta istry*, I was to observe all the fasts and pray ardently for my husband's long life, health and happiness. I was never to question any of his judgements, for he was my supreme lord and master and capable of making better decisions. Time and again, she quoted herself as the supreme *pativarta* because she would never have dreamt of marrying again, though her husband died after only a few years of marriage.

I was taken to see two films. Both were based on Sita—the idealised *pativarta* from the epic *Ramayana*. She hoped very much that I would bear sons and not daughters, as it was a tradition in their household. My father-in-law had four brothers and the other married brother of Darshan, who was residing in England at the time, had three sons. Besides, that was the least I could have done, as her son had been so very kind to me in marrying me. He was such a kind fellow. According to my mother-in-law, her son had taken pity on me, otherwise why marry an ugly-looking girl like me, when he had a select choice of offers from New Delhi, girls with fair skins, long flowing hair and ten times the dowry I had brought. All in all, she was very unhappy about the marriage.

It was my husband's aunt who had fostered him and it is to her that I refer as mother-in-law throughout this book. Her position was very dominating throughout my married life. No reference was ever made to Darshan's real mother, nor did she ever visit my parents in New Delhi.

One evening, when all the household chores had been done, Darshan took me for a walk around the town. We went to the water works and took some photographs. I asked him if there were any fields of mustard. Just outside the town, as far as the eye could see, the mustard was in full bloom. I remember standing at the edge of that field for hours, taking in the view and reflecting over the last few days' events. It was a very strange kind of household in that there was a mixture of the old and the new.

Next day, Darshan and I went to Delhi. Inder-Jeet and Sweety kept me busy with questions. They thought the world of their *jeeja ji* (brother-in-law). At bedtime, Sweety who was seven at the time, declared that no one but she had a right to talk to her brother-in-law. He was going to read her a bedtime story and she wanted to sleep right next to him.

Babuji called me into his study after everyone had settled down to one thing or another after the evening meal.

'What is this I hear about you joining Lady Harding Medical College here in Delhi?' he demanded.

'Darshan leaves for England in two weeks' time. I want to stay and finish my medical studies. That was the agreement—you know about it.'

'There was no such promise made,' he said. 'We said that we'd look into the possibility of admission to a college in the Punjab. Darshan says that he hasn't the time to do that. He has asked me to look into the matter and I think you should leave with him for England. I can get the passports and other documents ready,' he told me in his authoritarian manner.

'You can't mean any of that. Both you and Darshan agreed! You know that my medical career is the most important thing in the whole wide world to me,' I said, trembling and sobbing. I clenched my fists and experienced a feeling of utter bewilderment and restlessness. He had lied. He had cheated me.

'Don't talk such nonsense. You are a wife now, and perhaps will be a mother soon too. What do you want with a career? Darshan will find you a job in England.'

'You chose the place, the ceremony, the man and pushed me round a holy book four times, but you can't decide my feelings. I hate you! I despise you! Going round that holy book did not make a relationship of the mind, of the soul. You sold me. Didn't you? Tell me, what did he offer you? Freed you of the burden of dowry? Is that what it was? Tell me . . . !'

So, it was truly all over. I was never to become a doctor. Were there more lies to come? Was I going to be anything, anybody? I cried myself to sleep that night with Inder-Jeet clinging to me tightly. England? The word kept ringing in my ears. I was beginning to hate it already and I had not even arrived there yet. One thing that gave me hope was that I had heard and read in women's magazines that the overall position of women in society seemed fairer and freer in England than in India. Only time could tell.

7

Arrival in England

By 7 April, it was settled that I would be leaving for England with Darshan. I had no choice in the matter. Between the two of them, Darshan and my father decided that this course of action was best. They were both afraid that I might take some steps to humiliate and shame them. For my part, I can remember feeling utterly confused, restless and broken. There was nowhere to run. I had no enthusiasm for the future, or for my new career as a wife. I went about all the chores mechanically. I packed into a suitcase some of my favourite books—*Gitanjali* (a book of poems by Rabindranath Tagore); Waris Shah's *Heer* (India's most romantic tragedy); Shelley and Keats and a volume of Shakespeare; *The Railway Children*, a precious possession, as it was one of the prizes I had received as my school's champion speaker; and a very old historical book of Guru Nanak's teachings, given to me by Maan Santo. Unfortunately, Darshan got very cross and I had to unpack them all as only very limited luggage was allowed on the plane. There were lots of gifts for his friends and relatives and these were far more important than any of my cherished memories. But those books had a special place in my heart.

'Don't be sentimental. Women are all the same. And I have told you once, you'll be able to buy whatever you want in England.'

Darshan told me to make a gift of some of my ornaments to my mother-in-law, primarily for safe-keeping and also to show my trust in her. He said that, once we were in England, he would load me with English ornaments. I gave Bibijee some of the ornaments. I felt very sorry for her in declining years. She should be with her son and be looked after and kept in comfort. Instead, we were both going to leave her soon. She would never get to know me as a daughter-in-law. I promised her that I would ask my father to look into the matter and use all his influence to get her an entry permit to come and join us.

I had hoped desperately that my brother, Param-Jeet, would come before I left. I had not seen him for two years. Now I was going away, maybe never to return. He had not come to Delhi—I thought he might arrive in Bombay. I kept praying hard for a meeting with my dear brother but it did not happen. It was from Bombay that we finally boarded the plane for England.

Darshan seemed to be a quiet, gentle sort of man. He kept telling me about the joys and comforts of England. I wanted very much to look and feel happy for his sake, but I could not conjure up any excitement for a strange land. My only memory, my only experience of England was through school texts about colonialism, about the Empire's greed and the imperialism that connected India with England spiritually and psychologically; and the appalling slave mentality of my father's generation. In terms of years, Darshan was as near my father's age as he was to me. My father was thirty-nine. Both my uncles were younger than my husband. By the standards of those days ten years was a big gap. Did Darshan have the same sort of mentality as my father? Superficially, he seemed modern and liberal-minded. Why didn't he display any feelings of sadness at having to leave India? Wasn't it a shame that, to better himself financially, he had had to leave behind home, parents, brothers and sisters and his country? All my feelings of personal enjoyment, contentment and peace were interwoven in hours and hours of evening walks in the city of New Delhi— my city, my home. Buddha Jayanti Park and the Mogul Gardens were the most beautiful parks in the whole world and as for my favourite haunt, the Qutub Minar, there was no parallel anywhere to its impressive stateliness. Now, overnight I was to become a *pardesi* (one who leaves her country to live abroad) and all this, this exile, was designed to save my Babuji's *izzat* (honour). He might never see me again. Did the thought disturb him? Perhaps it never occurred to him. He had satisfactorily completed one of the most important tasks of his life, that was all that mattered. My predicament, my fears, my apprehension of the future, were of no consequence.

As I sat waiting for our plane at the airport in Bombay, I watched hundreds of our village folk dressed in five to six layers of clothing in order to take with them as much as they could without arousing the suspicions of the Customs. The relatives who had come to see them off kept embracing them and crying. There were utterances and reassurances all around.

'I should be able to earn enough within a year. I will come back for a visit then.'

'I am assured of a very well-paid job. I'll send you money regularly,' another was comforting his parents.

'It's only a matter of two to three months. Once I'm settled, I'll send for you.' A young man was trying hard to get his new bride, who was in hysterics, to smile.

Darshan too, was constantly telling me about a whole host of friends who were waiting to see his bride.

'They have arranged a party for us, a reception. Of course, we will have to return their favours and give parties too.'

He went on to tell me about all those 'very friendly people' who had helped him to settle in England when he first went there. It seemed he had at least two dozen different relatives settled in England, dotted around the country.

My India, my poor land, where widespread bad weather and over-population had depleted the best of resources down to an emptiness. This poverty is in material terms only. The richness of cultural tradition, the hospitality and warm affectionate feelings extended to all, are not equalled in any other country in the world. The differing temperatures and climatic conditions produce such a variety of landscape from Pathankot in the far north down to Ooty in the south; the variety of trees and plants is unmatched anywhere else in the world. And the people, from red-faced giant Pathans and pink Kashmir maidens in the north, through various shades of brown in the plains down to black Madrasis in the south—you never saw a more multi-ethnic, multi-cultural and multi-racial country. All the major religions of the world and some pretty obscure ones too, are practised there.

I bowed my head and said a quiet prayer.

Daro Dewari pe hasrat ki nazar rakhte hain,
Khush raho aah ley vatan hum to safar karte hain.
My eyes shall look upon you from afar with sadness.
Be happy my beloved country, I have now become a
    traveller to distant lands.

Darshan came and sat by me after having been to fill some forms in at the customs. By now, I had realised the non-existence of any emotion which is supposed to engulf husband and wife when they are close. Though I had let him claim his conjugal rights I had felt myself freeze. I did not dislike his closeness, but I would close my eyes tight and pray for those moments to be over as quickly as possible. Afterwards, I had wanted to be sick. He had automatically assumed that my fear was the result of this experience being new, or maybe I was pregnant? I could not tell him that his physical nearness produced in me a cold, clammy numbness. No, it would not have been right to admit to such personal feelings!

The journey from Bombay to Kuwait was very uncomfortable. My ears gave me a lot of trouble and I kept feeling very sick in the plane. Also, I discovered that Darshan was a strict vegetarian. He said that if ever I felt like eating chicken or any meat, we could go to a restaurant, but it was never to be cooked at home.

On 12 April 1966 I arrived in England. It was snowing heavily. Though I felt cold, the sight of snow was absolutely delightful. Thick snowflakes, like bits of cotton wool, were-covering everything in sight. I do not think I had ever seen the sky so grey. People all looked alike, and sounded exactly the same. Even the clothes seem to be three shades only—blue, black or grey.

I remember my first impression of Darshan's room. Almost bare and unwelcoming, it had lino-covered floor and huge repetitive patterns on the walls. This was my first encounter with that revolutionary wall-covering, wallpaper. Earlier Darshan had told me that the aunt who had brought him up, his father's widowed sister, had married into and therefore adopted her late husband's religion—Arya Samaj—a Hindu sect of very ancient traditions. I was therefore not expecting a photo of Guru Nanak with garlands of fresh flowers around it, but there wasn't even a bronze or clay statue of the deity. Even the poorest of Indian homes would be adorned with some hand-made objects of craft. There was nothing. Oh yes! I forgot. I do remember a bunch of plastic flowers in a plastic vase and a picture calendar of some Indian film stars on the wall. There was hardly any sunlight. The little there could have been was cut off by a pair of grey nylon curtains. I have hated net curtains ever since.

'Could I see some of your books please?' I had asked Darshan.

'What books Bhabhiji (sister-in-law)? The last book we read was when we were in our middle school.' My brother-in-law Hardev was laughing loudly, looking across at Darshan. Then he told me that he, Hardev, had not attended school much, but Darshan had at least passed the Matriculation Exam. Did I dare ask if Darshan was a qualified accountant at all?

And that was the most incredible irony of it all. This man, who supposedly by virtue of being a Sikh and an accountant, had satisfied my father's requirements of a 'suitable husband for me', was brought up as an orthodox Hindu and was only an accounts clerk. I recalled Babuji's words, 'Whatever I do, will be for your best.'

Though I did not take to the town of Slough at all, certain aspects of living in England were at least intriguing. The honesty of the self-service system at the supermarkets was a complete novelty. Such a shopping phenomenon was unheard of in India at the time. The orderliness of the high street, the automatic process of people queuing up, the door-to-door delivery of milk and the efficiently packaged food, amazed me. I did not like the way Indian people lived though. The majority of Darshan's relatives and friends were from the Punjab. They were offended by my command of English and referred to me as *shehari ladki* (city girl) all the time. I was not to be one of them. Both men and women worked all hours, while young children stayed at home with elderly relatives and watched television all day.

Gradually it became clear that my husband had no house of his own. He was only hoping to buy one in partnership with his brother. The three of us lived in two rented rooms in Richmond Crescent, Slough. My brother-in-law Hardev lived on social security and us. All the time that he stayed with us, it was free board and lodging. I never managed to understand why Darshan didn't ask him to share the household expenses. We supported him fully, including his drinking and smoking. When I did question this state of affairs once I was told in very definite terms that, as I did not contribute financially to his upkeep personally, I should not grumble.

Despite my repeated requests, there was no definite proposal to start my medical studies. As time went by, I came to realise that Darshan was a thousand pounds in debt to various people and at least another thousand was owed to various catalogue agencies. I did not understand the way these mail order companies operated, but I could see the ease with which people could get into trouble as regards payment. When Darshan had gone to India, it was primarily to get his sister married. She had demanded a number of English goods—a tape recorder, transistor radio, camera, food mixer and a number of shirts and jumpers as part of her dowry. It was quite normal of her to expect this of her older brother. Darshan had bought all these from various catalogues and now money was owed.

I also became aware of the desperate need for me to find a job, as money was owed to the *rationwalah*, as we called the grocer, to the milkman and the landlady. When the television company came and took the television away as at least eight months rent was outstanding, we had the first of the many ugly rows that were to follow. I had begun to resent bitterly the lies that had been told. Darshan reminded me constantly that I was a rejected girl and that no one would have married me. He had supposedly rescued me from a fate worse than death. I was supposed to be grateful to him for the rest of my life, and not shame my father any more. Later in the day he came home drunk and demanded quite forcibly that I should give him all my ornaments. I had no choice but to do so. I was allowed to keep a ring and chain which my parents had given to me. The ornaments were sold in order to pay off the 'pool' money for the rest of the year. Some of the Indians living in Slough had formed a 'pool' into which they all paid £25 every month, and every month one person was allowed to draw out the total money and use it for his or her personal need. It was a good way of making a fair amount of cash available for the needy. Different criteria were used to determine the need. Once a person had had their turn, they would obviously have to wait a year and also make sure that the payments were kept up.

We lived in Slough for eighteen months. Every day that passed I heard many stories of women in similar circumstances as me. A lot of them had been brought to England under false pretences. As long as a marriage could be arranged, it did not matter how many lives were ruined. Every day, I met many sisters who were living embodiments of the Indian woman's philosophy of 'tolerance, acceptance, hope and devotion'. In the agony of the realisation of what my future held I often cried myself to sleep.

It was July 1966. I can remember praying a lot for a child. All else was lost. Perhaps a child would be my salvation. It certainly would have been a good reason for living. I was beginning to believe that, as everything and everyone I had loved and cared for had been taken away from me, perhaps I was never going to be blessed with a child. Maybe God was punishing me for not responding to my husband the way a wife should.

At the beginning of July I started my first job in England as a laboratory technician at Burnham Grammar School, Burnham, Bucks. By the end of July I was pregnant. The baby was due in April 1967: life was just around the corner. My new life was just beginning.

8

Burnham Grammar School and Khushwant's Arrival

I went to work at Burnham Grammar School as a laboratory technician with a song in my heart and my spirits uplifted, and I was constantly being told by colleagues that I glowed all over with health. I looked forward to a future full of promise. Destiny's unknown hand had thrown a life-line to rescue me.

The time spent at Burnham Grammar was a happy one. The work was neither hard nor interesting, but it kept me occupied. I enjoyed being with children and teenagers. In those days it was quite a novelty to be an Indian in such a situation: I was the only coloured person in the school. I remember with tremendous fondness the kindness of Mr Butler, Mr Chudley, Mr Lomas and Mrs Butler, all the science teachers for whom I worked. It was a nice happy atmosphere. The children were always inquisitive, and three of the sixth formers became almost like friends as I used to find great joy in helping them with their experiments. It wasn't long since I had done many of those myself at college. This was also the place where one of the nicest attitudes of the English came to be a part of my experience. I felt and enjoyed their kindness towards me as a pregnant woman. As there were no elders in the family to give advice, I was grateful too for the excellent medical care under the National Health Service.

The senior laboratory technician, though a bit bossy, was always ready to teach me anything I wanted to learn about the job. I must have been at that school for about six months when Mr Chudley mentioned just as a matter of interest about teacher training courses. From then on, the more we talked about teacher training, the more enthusiastic I became about giving it a go. It was foolish to go on contemplating the idea, the dream, of becoming a doctor. It was well and truly over.

I wrote to my parents several times informing them of the reality of the situation. Once, I wrote a long letter to my father congratulating him on the length of the punishment that he had designed for me. Time and again they both wrote back to say that it was *parmatma ka hukum* (God's will), *mere karam* (my fate) and *karmon ke khel* (the games of destiny). They wrote to me letters full of *shabads* or hymns from the Adi Granth, (the holy book of the Sikhs), and told me to seek solace in praising the Lord and praying. They pleaded for me to stay obedient to Darshan and to keep on sending money home to my in-laws. In the end, I simply gave up trying to explain to my parents about the debts; about our living conditions, and my anxieties about the baby; about the persistent and continuous stream of debt collectors. Mother had written 'Turn to Guru Nanak's teachings my daughter. Guru Nanak writes, *"Aapne hathein apna aape hi kaj savariay"*.' Roughly translated, it means that you must take destiny in your own hands and put right what is wrong. These lines have stayed with me all my life.

As all attempts had failed to get my husband to sit down and work our economic situation out properly, I decided to give up expecting anything, and simply to live from day to day and do my best. Perhaps it was some time during those uncertain and insecure days that a kind of metamorphosis of my personality began. Almost everything that I had imagined my husband to be was a figment of the imagination. For months I tried hard to get him to work out a routine which would make it possible to share the household chores. Like most Asian men, he considered the idea of doing housework degrading and hurtful to his male ego. His answer was always the same: 'It's a woman's job.'

The work at Burnham Grammar gave me economic independence. At least the rent was paid and there was food in the house. Month-by-month, I collected clothes for the baby. Because of the debts, it was quite clear that I would have to contribute financially for a very long time. Darshan could not find a better job because he was not qualified and with all his commitments back home, there would never be the security I was looking for. He was an accounts clerk at a builders' firm and continually told lies to hide the truth about not being a chartered accountant.

It was during one of those days at Australia Road, where we had moved in July 1966, that Darshan first raised his hand to me. The kitchen in the flat was a dark, dingy, grimy place. We rented the flat from an Indian family and apart from us there were two other lodgers in that fairly ordinary, three-bedroomed terraced house. I was standing at the kitchen sink doing some dishes. My eyes fell on what looked like half a rotten lemon by the dustbin on the floor. I picked it up and put it with the rest of the rubbish from the washing-up on the work-top, to be thrown away later. As I stood there, within a matter of minutes, I saw the slimy, rotten piece of lemon move. Startled and numbed by fear at first, my next reaction was to flick the rubbish off the work-top. Darshan heard my scream and, as he realised that it was a slug, burst out laughing. I remember shaking and yelling, 'What the hell are you laughing at? That thing has scared me half out of my mind. I hate this place. I hate living in this horribly dirty house.'

He pushed me out of the way still laughing and saying how silly I was to let a harmless thing like a slug frighten me so. I pushed back and struggled to get back to my washing up. Tears veiling my eyes, I asked if he would pick the rubbish up for me. Instead, he laughed even louder, told me to do it myself and to come to my senses. I picked up some of the rubbish and threw it at him. He slapped me and I fell on to the edge of a chair. I was seven months pregnant.

I started to shout, yell and scream and said that he was a cruel brute, that he had perhaps killed the baby. His response was to leave the house. Minutes later he had returned with his aunt and uncle from Richmond Crescent. The aunt was very kind and gradually talked me out of my incoherent state of mind. I cried a lot that day. Darshan's unsympathetic and indifferent attitude had foretold the future even more clearly. He rebuked me for making a big issue out of nothing and for not having enough self-control. Though they are totally harmless, my fear of slugs has stayed with me to this day.

Back home in India, in the last days of her pregnancy, a young mother would go back to her parent's home to be cajoled and cared for. Instead, there I was in a miserable, gloomy house, where no one could really give a damn, where the sun never seemed to shine and spring was many months away.

Khushwant arrived on 24 April 1967 at the maternity home in Farnham Common, Bucks. He was the most beautiful, most wonderful miracle to happen to me. My husband and my mother-in-law were over the moon. Letters came, presents came. I was not such a bad daughter-in-law after all. I was not an ill-omen. The family prestige was kept up. It was a son. At seven-and-a-half pounds, with a glorious head of hair, my baby was a picture of health. Khush (happiness) Khushwant (a source of happiness), we named him, after the writer of the same name. I remember well how we had gone to the Royal Albert Hall to listen to Khushwant Singh's talk on the 500th Anniversary of Guru Nanak's birth. It was there that the name had been decided if it was a boy.

I held him in my arms and felt new life surge into me. I had a reason to live, the nicest reason of all, life itself. I promised him silently that I would try to be the best mother in the whole wide world and would never let him down. He was the beginning of a new life for me. I sang the Ashabad from the Adi Granth with joy in my heart—'*Diya prem ka patola pat dhakan ko*'. 'Thank you Lord for giving a bundle of love to save my honour.'

Darshan's joy knew no bounds. He, his brother and friends spent pounds on drink every night and celebrated, for he was now equal to his brother and uncle. Both his brother and uncle had sons. He had promised me that when I returned from the maternity home it would be into a flat of our own in Gerrards Cross. He kept his promise. It was a one-bedroomed flat in Midcross Lane, Chalfont Common. Darshan and his brother Hardev decorated it beautifully. The wallpaper had an enchanting peacock design. Everything was new. Everything was mine. I did not have to share anything any more, not even the cooker. And there was even a small garden.

Motherhood fascinated me. I took great delight in watching Kushwant's every move. I could see now why we refer to the earth as 'mother earth'. I had managed to grow a miracle of my very own. To me, it has always been the most incredible marvel, the birth of a new life, perhaps because it was the only emotion I was free to display without opposition, and with very satisfying rewards in return. Whatever the reasons, motherhood filled my life with happiness and contentment. I didn't mind the financial struggles any more and I was planning and preparing to do the teacher training course Mr Chudley had suggested. I was going to provide for my son as best I could.

During those days homesickness was a big problem. The thoughts of home and how proud my mother would have been of her first grandchild. My mother would have made a delicious preparation of *dabra*—a mixture of sultanas, ghee, grain flour or semolina, and sugar to help me regain my strength. Both sets of grandparents would have exchanged gifts of money and clothes such as turbans. An *Akhand Path* (a non-stop reading of the holy book) would be done, at the end of which *ladoos* (sweetmeats) and *parsad* of various kinds, even *langar*, a meal of dal, chapatis, rice and dahi would be distributed to all who could come.

And in India we would have had a proper naming ceremony. To mark the start of this celebration, an open prayer would be said. The atmosphere is one of joyous celebration. There is *Kirtan* (singing of *shabads*) with accompaniment. A token gift, *sava rupeya*, is made along with a beautifully adorned *rumalla*, a square piece of cloth to cover the holy book. The Adi Granth is opened, and the first word of the first *shabad* on the left-hand page is told to the parents. The name of the child must begin with the first letter of the first word. All present are at liberty to make suggestions. Once the name is decided, the master of the ceremony will say '*Jo bole so nihal*', 'Whoever says his name shall feel fulfilled,' and the congregation would reply, '*Sat siri akal*', 'God is the only Truth'. This is a kind of approval. I could not help feeling a deep sense of loss as, instead of this beautiful ceremony, I said a quiet prayer and registered Khushwant's name at the Registry of Births and Deaths.

Eleven weeks were over almost in the blink of an eye. I had to go back to my job at Burnham Grammar. I resented leaving Khush with a child-minder very much. Back home, I had never even heard of the word. A child was brought up amongst grandparents, uncles, cousins; rich in social and emotional interaction. Perhaps this was one of the best virtues of the extended family system, creating a most loving and secure atmosphere to grow up in. Darshan was not too concerned; he was already familiar with the system and, anyway, the child-minder's house was barely twenty yards away from his work. He was very confident that everything would be fine, that my fears were unfounded. After all, I'd be with the baby in the evenings and during school holidays. The majority of Asians living in Slough and Birmingham had to do the same. 'But I want to bring my baby up myself,' was all I could think of, over and over again. I wished to God he had once expressed some regret, some concern. Where had the joy of becoming a father gone? Evaporated overnight?

I hated the parting scene from Khush every morning. As I'd dress him, I am sure he must have sensed my anguish. He'd cling to me and cry. I started getting up at five o'clock so that I could light the fire and do other morning chores before he got up. I then had a good hour and a half to spend with him and calm us both down. But the thought of leaving my baby with a stranger produced pangs of pain all day.

It must have been in the early months of 1968 when one afternoon I received a telephone call at school from Darshan to say that Khush had been hurt and was it possible for me to come to the child-minder's house straightaway? Panic-stricken I arrived at the child-minder's to find Khush sitting in a high chair, smothered in blood and with his lower lip swollen. Apparently he had bitten a glass beaker while drinking from it. What was a ten-month-old baby doing with a glass beaker? The child-minder did not answer, but told me to wait. Khush was at the other end of the room. In the middle were four adults having their dinner. I think I must have annoyed the child-minder with my persistent demands to take my baby. As I tried to reach for him, she picked him up and literally threw him at me and slapped my face and said, 'Take your bloody child away! I didn't want to look after a black bastard anyway.' Shocked, as if someone had jabbed me with a knife, angry, hurt and bitter, I saw Darshan just standing there. He did absolutely nothing. I didn't say a word but put Khush gently into the pram and walked the whole three miles home from Gerrards Cross to Chalfont Common. I shall never forget the humiliation of it all.

During those formative years of my life as a mother, Mr Childs' presence was most comforting. Some eighty years old, my landlord was an independent, cheerful and caring sort of man. I used to think how these three qualities would make a man or woman the kind of person one would want to spend one's life with. He was like a father I never had. I used to arrive home about five o'clock. The biology teacher, Mrs Butler, kindly gave me a lift back home every day. Within a quarter of an hour of Khush and me coming home, he'd call from the bottom of the stairs, 'Sharan! Tea is ready love!' To Khush it was a signal to crawl down the stairs at top speed into Mr Childs' lap, where biscuits and a cup of warm milky tea awaited him. I think now that they both filled a gap in each other's lives. For the four years that I knew Mr Childs he never once forgot to make the tea for me, or stopped showing his daily concern for Khush. In 1971 he died; I felt a very deep loss.

My time at Burnham Grammar had come to an end. I had sat two three-hour papers in english and maths at Newland Park College of Education, Chalfont St Giles, and secured admission to do a three-year teacher training course there starting in September 1968.

We had found an older lady, Mrs Lane, to look after Khush. She was not a registered child-minder, but came highly recommended via the local postmaster. She had a nine-year-old son of her own who kept Khush company like an older brother. The arrangement worked very well until Khush was three years old and went to a full-time nursery school. He has very pleasant memories of the nursery school, Cheena House, to this day.

For myself I only had one dream, to study diligently for my Certificate of Education and to qualify as a teacher. Those were the days when multicultural or anti-racist teaching was unheard of. In Slough and High Wycombe, two of the schools I visited during my studies, the authority's policies of 'bussing' black school children (dispersing them into schools outside their catchment area to avoid a 'concentration' of black children in any one school) and treating 'immigrants' as problems, were to lay the foundations of a growing awareness of racism in me. During my visits to schools in Slough and High Wycombe, I met many Asian women, some of them had teaching qualifications from India. Here, in England, those were not recognised and they could only find employment as welfare assistants or nursery and infant school teachers. I could feel their struggle but had no answers. I often thought of the women that I had met as I tried to study while caring for Khush and playing the quadrupal role of wife, mother, housewife and career woman, like millions and millions of invisible women.

9

The Growing Rift

Despite all the social reform movements in India, particularly Mahatma Gandhi's revolutionary approach to women's role in society, the suppression of women goes on, comparable in my view only to slavery. Mahatma Gandhi wrote year after year in the journal *Young India* seeking to inspire women to eradicate their 'humiliation and ill-treatment'. If the 'laws of discipline' were broken in a marriage, and there was physical violence, a woman had every right to break that bond. He wrote, 'If divorce was the only alternative I should not hesitate to accept it, rather than interrupt my moral progress . . .'—*Young India*, 15 December 1921.

In Gandhiji's opinion, women had to shed their traditional inferiority, refuse to be objects of lust and take up an equal role in the fight for freedom and social justice. In his view, women were more competent to lead a struggle on non-violent lines, for nature had endowed them with greater power to love, endure and suffer. Yet, despite his most compassionate writings, most of his ideas remain unfulfilled. In the name of *izzat*, a girl is still taught by her mother to suffer silently, to walk at least two paces behind her husband, to cover part or the whole of her face in the presence of all the males of her husband's household, and to put herself at the bottom of the list as regards family welfare.

I too continued to wait and hope that through silent suffering I would be able to attain a measure of harmony in my marriage. Darshan would, I felt, some day need Khush and me, need our love and our friendship. It was obvious that his feelings of duty and his obligations towards his family back home in Slough were the only real feelings he ever had. If his relatives in India asked for money over and above the regular monthly money order we sent, Darshan would get very agitated. At first he would be annoyed about his parents and brothers not managing their finances carefully. Then he would sit up late at night figuring out ways to obtain money to send home. It did not seem to matter to him how many finance companies we owed money to. Money was always borrowed under our joint names. For years I was foolishly convinced by him that by so doing, he was treating me as his partner. He was, I must admit, pretty clever with words in those days. Money borrowed jointly means joint responsibility. Those financial obligations were crippling. The queue of debt collectors on the doorstep started to become obvious. At first, I was told that they were relatives from Slough who had recently visited India and had brought news for us. Gradually, I became suspicious; their voices were loud and sounded angry, not at all the friendly conversations one would expect from visitors. I would be sitting in the adjoining room, with Khush on my lap or playing nearby, simply listening and praying for these people to go away, jumping to commands every so often to supply tea and *pakoras* (an Indian savoury dish). A debt is like a venomous snake, a python, or perhaps like cancer, eroding away one's insides, gradually but surely. The only way we could get rid of our debts was by borrowing money from elsewhere. The insecurity that this produced was debilitating.

In the early months of Khushwant's childhood I was not able to look on employment as a means of upholding my own self-respect and dignity as well as being a stable means of income. In fact, I carried on suffering under the illusion that my husband's role as a breadwinner was the most important and that my income was to be merely supplementary. Going to college for teacher training was, however, of immense personal consequence, if only to uphold my badly bruised ego at the time.

It was sometime during those harsh, insecure days that I became aware of a number of attitudes. It was so easy for me to want to find expansion and expression in Khushwant's childhood. Perhaps, to a certain extent, all parents seek fulfilment of their unconsummated aims and aspirations in their children. For an Indian mother, it is made even easier by the basic philosophy of a son being the provider in one's old age. I could see now how, in the absence of the very basic tool of economic independence, the majority of Indian women drift into a submissive state of fatalism. The burden of dependence is very cumbersome. The tentacles cling so tenaciously that escape is unthinkable. A son then becomes a mother's complete world. But I was determined to become self-reliant; I wanted to shoulder all responsibilities together with my husband. I was going to make a good marriage. After all, we three had only each other. I, for one, did not have any relatives in Britain; my husband and my son were the two most important people to me. I wanted to learn each and every skill that was needed to make us self-sufficient and happy.

However, as the years rolled by, my husband's indifference towards both of us grew. It was almost as if we did not exist. Every weekend, by the time he had made his weekly trip to Slough to exchange news of 'back home' with his brother and countless other relatives, there was no time left for us as a family. I would argue most emphatically that Khush and I needed him, needed his time for chores around the house. He would constantly ignore my pleas and would usually end the argument by labelling me as a cruel, selfish, heartless woman who did not like his brothers and sisters and who therefore was an unworthy daughter-in-law. Unworthy, that is, of his parents' love, who were so kind to express their love for me in all their letters.

A couple of incidents reflect the growing rift between us, and how his traditional dogma kept coming between us. Perhaps I should not put the total blame on tradition, for Darshan's own personality and character also came into play.

I believed quite firmly that once my husband's debts were paid he would naturally want to provide for Khush and me. This was the natural expectation for me as a married woman, that he would provide a good home for our son. I used to dream how, when Khushwant grew up, father and son would together indulge in all the usual activities, such as playing football, swimming, kite flying, and so on, while I would watch. My job as a mother would be to fill Khushwant's world with the best literature from both cultures, to give religious instruction and to teach him the traditional values to develop a staunch character. Meanwhile, I enjoyed watching my young son grow up. I did not want Khush to be disadvantaged in any way. I therefore set out to find out about all the playtime activities of English children. Together, Khush and I explored the vast pre-school world of games, nursery rhymes and children's literature.

Penny Jones and Annabel Curry, my two very close friends, were the models from which I learnt to shape my own role as a mother. I was in my third year at college. My sources of income were strictly limited. I had a grant from the local County Council, a lot of which had to go on paying the child-minder. My friend Annabel was very kind and bought me most of the books I needed for college. I did not consider it beneath me to accept second-hand toys, sheets, and items of clothing for Khush and myself from any source. It was either that or go without. Annabel was like an aunt for Khush. She was a lady of means and kept Khush well supplied with some of the nicest educational toys and games. I was grateful for her presence in my life, for her company and constant caring. Though she would often scold Darshan in a very diplomatic manner, she never tried to give advice or interfere in any way.

Khushwant was about two years old and needed a small garden to play in. It was becoming very tiring and tedious to walk him to the park which was some mile-and-a-half away. We could not afford to buy turf. There were two alternatives. We could have dug, raked and seeded our patch and waited for the grass to grow—my landlord, Mr Childs, an expert gardener, was happy to teach us the basic know-how of making a lawn. The other alternative involved a lot of physical labour, but meant an instant lawn. I was very doubtful of my physical strength in taking on this task single-handed, but knew that Darshan and I could easily do it together. Penny and Richard Jones, our friends who lived half a mile away, were going to dig up some turf from their back garden to make a patio. They had offered us this turf, provided we made our own arrangements to move it to our house. There was no car or van available, but twenty or so trips with a wheelbarrow which they could lend us would shift the turf.

Darshan wouldn't hear of it. He rebuked me and told me in very clear terms that I was lowering myself to the status of a 'beggar', and that if I was going to go through this 'begging', I'd have to do so by myself and he wanted no part of it. The fact that Penny and Richard were only going to throw the turf on to a rubbish heap was irrelevant in his eyes. He was very angry and hurled all kinds of verbal abuse at me. He wasn't at all willing to discuss the fact that Khush had nowhere to play, that he was growing up and desperately needed space. A one-bedroomed flat with no garden was not exactly an idyllic haven for a little toddler.

As Darshan settled himself to watch the midday football, his objections made me even more determined to complete the task single-handed. I sat Khush in his pram with his favourite toys around him, and left him with Mr Childs, who remarked, 'Where's that no-good husband of yours?' Perhaps he understood, perhaps he didn't, but seeing the tears in my eyes, he said nothing else. All that afternoon, he kept providing me with cups of tea as well as making sure that I was laying the turf properly. In the evening, shoulders aching, blisters on hands, I stood back and proudly admired my work. The best part was seeing Khush toddling around kicking a football.

As time went by, the need to survive taught me skills which as a teenager I was led to believe were a man's domain. I believe now that most jobs around the house can be done with considerable accuracy provided one is prepared to have a go and persevere. 'Not bad for a woman' used to irritate me. Now, I put it down to pure male chauvinism and arrogance. I have taught myself to produce quite impressive results with all kinds of decorating and maintenance jobs. I have seen many of my European counterparts do the same, very skilfully and successfully. It is a very satisfying pursuit indeed. Not only does it give pleasure, but it also makes one a far more capable and confident person.

In all my sixteen years of marriage, my husband never did any gardening or house maintenance. His answer used to be, 'You should get someone else to do such menial tasks on a paid basis or do them yourself. Don't bother me with such minor problems.' Perhaps in later life he would come to regret his lack of any hobbies or interests. I had begun to create an independent existence for myself. It seemed that if I was to succeed in achieving a reasonable standard of living, it was up to me. I couldn't even tell if it hurt Darshan's ego to see me do jobs peculiarly categorised as a man's domain. He never expressed any definite views, directly or indirectly. On the other hand, to give help with what was in his eyes 'a woman's job' was undesirable and in his opinion would have turned him into a hen-pecked husband, an object of mockery.

Darshan and I were two of the most incompatible personalities, emotionally, physically and mentally. There was no companionship, no friendliness between us. I found him a very boring person, interested only in the past—the golden days of his youth—and his people back home. He found me, as he often used to point out, exasperating.

'Why can't you accept things as they are? You're always looking for perfection.'

'No, I'm not, I just want to improve our standards. I don't wish to stagnate.'

There was no chance of us going back to India and finding a home, either with his family or mine. As England was going to be home for the rest of our lives, I felt it was only realistic to put my effort into building a secure future for ourselves here.

Despite the fact that the true circumstances of his family had been revealed, he would never stop boasting. In this he was, as the cliché says, his own worst enemy. Our squabbles, explosions really, used to be loud in those days. Poor Khush! He was often a witness to my stormy, bilingual displays of temper. I used to plead with my husband to stop living in his spectacular 'fantasy world'. The bare fact was that he had fallen deeply into debt, whilst keeping his parents in a constant state of delusion as to his wealth. His staggering lies about riches would surely misfire one day. My optimism was beginning to wear thin. I was drifting into a world of my own—for the sake of self-preservation and survival.

Khushwant was about three years old. Darshan wanted his Bibijee (the aunt who had adopted him) to come and live with us. I was convinced too that he would settle down to a proper family life if Bibijee was with us. A lot of the financial and emotional frustration would end. I wasn't sure in my mind about how she would cope with life here, but my doubts wouldn't have made any difference, he would have coerced me into agreement anyway. So in 1969, we sent Bibijee the necessary documents, the affidavit and the ticket.

My father agreed to look into the matter personally. All was arranged. In order to ascertain that nothing should go wrong, Bibijee was briefed thoroughly by my father before her interview with the British High Commission. It was the year when Mr Enoch Powell's prediction about 'rivers of blood' was very fresh in people's minds; it wouldn't be going too far to say that the media had predicted anarchy, if immigration continued at its massive rate. The British government at the time had reacted quickly to pass new legislation, and entry permits were very difficult to get hold of.

Bibijee was a widow, totally dependent upon Darshan. She was perfectly entitled to come and live with us, her only family. Only there was a hitch. Everyone had overlooked the fact that she had never completed any legal adoption deeds. The entry permit was denied. In the eyes of the law, she was just a widowed aunt.

My father approached every judge, every M.P. he knew, to straighten out the mess, but even the highest authority could not have passed a new law concerning adoption just to suit my husband. My husband wrote desperate letters to our local M.P., regretfully without any results. It infuriated him to the point of paranoia. He had countless meetings with officials at the Indian High Commission.

I am afraid I did not feel sorry for him. He had always boasted of being educated, having contacts in high places and being very knowledgeable about the law. It was his own fault. Another of his illusions had been shattered. His attitude was essentially absurd: he blamed everyone else, including my father and me. Though my father was never my most favourite person, this was one time when he had tried his very best to pull all strings known to him for my sake. I genuinely believe that this episode alone was responsible for the gradually worsening relationship between Darshan and his Bibijee. Though he never let her want financially, in later years she sued him in a court of law over their joint property which he had helped to build, furnish and maintain for well over twenty-five years.

Bibijee and I never got to know each other personally. I wrote to her regularly, enclosing photographs depicting Khushwant's progress. In all those years, she wrote to me directly only twice: once when Khushwant was born and once when I was in the middle of divorce proceedings. All her letters were always addressed to Darshan, with the same single line at the end for me: 'We hope that your wife is happy and well.'

By 1970, our financial commitments were so steep that nearly all of Darshan's salary was swallowed up by the repayment of debts. When I read the contents of the letter from the tax office which had arrived by recorded delivery, I simply wanted to hide away and die. Until then I had let Darshan take care of all our tax matters. As he was an accountant by profession, I had accepted the fact that he knew best. I was not aware that, ever since his arrival in 1962, he had been making false claims for a wife and two children. When he married me, he had declared to the Home Office that, as his first wife had died, I was his second wife. Therefore he claimed for seven dependents in all, myself, his three children, Bibijee, and his real mother and father.

The tax claim was made on the advice of Darshan's elderly relatives living in Slough. Apparently, they all did this in order to boost their earnings. 'After all, rich people all over the world did it', was the justification. Exactly how the tax office's investigation brought it to light, I do not know, but a general amnesty was declared for all those immigrants who had evaded tax in this way—so long as they were to come forward voluntarily and pay back the sum owed. All in all, for the period from 1963 to 1971, Darshan owed £500. His brother Hardev and the other relatives did not want to get involved. Of course, they would have loved to help, but they had their own families. (Extended families are commended to help each other in times of crisis. Why did some of this help never come our way?) If my husband was not to accept his folly voluntarily, when found out, imprisonment would have been inevitable. We would have had to stop sending money home.

Darshan was not very keen to write to India explaining the details of the situation, so I did. The reply that I received was a clear indication of their total indifference to our anxiety, our suffering. They had not bothered to understand the explanatory notes. They were very cross that I was now taking decisions for their son; I was a callous brute of a daughter-in-law. Clearly, I did not fear God and was quite happy to see my in-laws become beggars on the street. 'As it is, the money that you send us is barely enough for clothes. When Darshan's sisters come to visit us on festivals, we are unable to provide them with the gifts required from parents on such occasions. *'Hamari naak katti dekh ke tum khush hote ho?'* 'You are an educated girl. Are you happy to see us socially disgraced? We had expected sympathy and understanding from you, honour and decency; instead you are determined to snatch our food from us.' And so it went on.

One must remember that, on average, there is at least one festival per month when it is customary in India for the families to meet socially and exchange gifts, in addition to the ceremonies surrounding births, deaths, and marriages. That night when we sat down to our evening meal, Darshan pushed his food away saying that, while we ate such a hearty meal, his parents might be hungry. This over-exaggeration of his parents' plight was, needless to say, a very simple ploy to gain my sympathy. In those days I tended to blame myself a lot. Almost every event like this I saw as an act of God to punish me. I did not deserve to be a part of Darshan's family. I felt embittered, yet confused, and lost, so lost. Was it my destiny to stand alone? Somehow, Darshan managed to make me feel responsible for it all.

Here it is important to outline the circumstances in my in-laws' household. My father-in-law was the joint owner of a flour and sugar mill which supplied them with the four basic necessities of life, butter, flour, sugar and rice. The house, one of the largest properties in the village, was Darshan's and Bibijee's joint property. His three brothers and his real parents lived there too. The money that we sent was only meant to support Bibijee, yet time and again we received letters confirming that the money was used to keep his brother Amrik in cigarettes and drink. Term after term, Amrik failed his exams, but my husband was determined that, whatever the cost, his brother must complete his B.A. studies. Instead of the usual three years, it took him five years to qualify.

I gave up trying to figure out any solution with Darshan. I used to work as a nursing auxiliary at Amersham Hospital during college holidays. During term-time I took up the only job that was suitable, that of office cleaner, four evenings a week. It was an evening job and while it lasted, I saw even less of Khush. Darshan objected strongly to the nature of the job, but didn't seem to mind the money. For four evenings' work, two hours per evening, I brought home £6.00 a week, which in 1970 was enough to supply food for the three of us.

Perhaps one day I would have paid the price in full for my guilt? At some time, during the course of those ugly days, I must have stopped relating to my husband. Khush and I were a separate, meaningless entity to him. Though I had not yet completed my course, I was already independent financially. I never asked for any contribution from him towards household expenses. He paid the rent, the gas and the electricity bill. In return he got my services. That was how I viewed my marriage. That was the stark reality of it all.

10

A Visit Home

Gold Hill Common reminded me of Simla in India. Long walks by myself in its serenity to shake off the melancholy of my marital confusion had become part of my everyday routine. Homesickness was still a big problem. I missed the colourful festivals, especially Baisakhi, Republic Day and Deepawali. Of so many Indian festivals, I loved these three the best.

Baisakhi is the most important day in the Sikh calendar. It marks the beginning of the harvest reaping in April. At the Baisakhi gathering in 1699, Guru Gobind Singh laid the foundations of the *Khalsa-Panth* (the Sikh brotherhood). On Republic Day, gaily decorated floats from various parts of India take part in a five-hour procession, along with schoolchildren and the military, to celebrate the country's anniversary of independence. Deepawali is the festival of lights which marks the end of the *Dussehra* celebrations. During the *Dussehra*, dramas and plays are enacted, and tall effigies of the evil King Ravan are filled with fireworks and burnt. The return of Rama after fourteen years in exile is celebrated by exchanging presents, and by gala illuminations with electric lights, candles or wick lamps.

It was October 1971 and the festival of Diwali. I organised a small feast and invited our Asian as well as English friends. Of course, I would never have been allowed this if Darshan's relatives from Slough had been excluded. I made lots of Indian vegetarian dishes, an English trifle and cakes. The first part of the evening went smoothly, everyone narrating nostalgic memories. The conversation then turned to the changing roles of men and women. The Indian couple, Surinder and Kaajal, lived together, though they were not married. They were both at work, and therefore shared all the household chores.

'I have never even washed a cup. The kitchen is my Sharan-Jeet's domain. She wouldn't allow me to enter it. Would you darling?' said Darshan proudly.

'If I asked you for help in housework, you would either utter some abuse or tell me to leave it till later, anyway.'

'That's not true. I boil the eggs for breakfast every morning. And didn't I cut the grass for you the other day?' Darshan's voice was getting louder.

'For me?' I was equally indignant.

'*Chup kar maan-chod!*' 'How dare you waggle your tongue at me in front of my guests?'

At this Surinder and Brian (our English friend) told Darshan that they considered his attitude to be totally unfair and unreasonable. He told them to mind their own business and not put such innovatory ideas into his wife's head.

Where was the pleasant evening that I had envisaged?

After everybody had left, Darshan rebuked me and said that I had encouraged Surinder to speak out against him. In future, I should show the proper respect accorded to a husband. What kind of a pointless argument was this? Everything that went wrong was automatically my fault. What a nonsensical farce this Diwali celebration had been!

My thoughts turned towards home once again. For Sikhs, Diwali has a different meaning. It celebrates Guru Hargobind's release from the Gwalior Fort where he had been imprisoned by the emperor Jahangir, along with fifty-two Hindu princes. At the end of a day full of exciting celebrations, as mother tucked us up in bed, she would tell us the story of Guru Hargobind's escape. Guruji had refused freedom unless the emperor would grant the same to the Hindu princes. The emperor had replied that as many as could hold onto Guruji's cloak and pass through the narrow tunnel of the fort would be allowed to go. Guruji had a long cloak made with lots of tassels and thus allowed all the princes to be freed. I told Khush this story, but somehow, it all seemed out of place.

I was starting to have doubts about my ability to impart proper religious instruction to Khush. Darshan had declared his agnostic views loud and clear. He did not wish to participate in our morning prayers. It is instructed by the Adi Granth clearly that one must practice religion publicly in *sangat* (congregation) as well as privately. I was brought up with this training but, though Darshan was quite glad to take us to Slough to attend the Sunday worship, I was always very hesitant to go. After the worship, visiting various relatives was inevitable regardless of any personal arrangements. The other nearest Gurudwara was held in London and as yet we had no transport. The moving finger had written my destiny for me. Was there a way to carve out a niche for myself in all this? I thought of the lines by Omar Khayyam:

> O love! Could thou and I with fate conspire
> To scrap this sorry scheme of things entire
> Should not we shatter it to bits and then
> Remould it near to our heart's desire?

Both my mother and Cousin Malkeet wrote very sympathetic and encouraging letters. Mother sent best wishes on all festive occasions, writing in detail about how she had said prayers on my behalf. Every year she would plant my favourite flowers and vegetables, and every year she held an *Akhand Path* for Khushwant's well-being on his birthday.

It was with my mother and Cousin Malkeet that I communicated at an emotional level. Cousin Malkeet understood the baffling situation that was tearing me apart; he understood my quest to find a new way for self-fulfilment. An officer in the air force, he was also a very sensitive poet of no mean reputation. In my state school in India, ironically, it was English literature that I studied. India's educational system had not begun to recognise its own poets and writers—another attitude inherited from the days of the British Raj. I remember how, as a child during the long summer-holiday period, Veer Malkeet would read me Ghalib, Iqbal and other famous Punjabi and Urdu poets, while I would narrate my favourite verses from Shelley, Keats and Milton. In all his letters to me, he wrote poems to inspire me:

> The smile of a child can disperse
> The clouds of anguish and misery.
> The rising sun can give new strength
> To our shattered thoughts and agony.
> Let the brimming stream give you hope

The flying birds fly your heart
Let the colours of the sky at sunset
Dye your spirit and your heart.

Letters came regularly from my sisters Inder-Jeet and Sweety. Inder-Jeet in particular missed me desperately. As she stepped into her adolescent years, the memory of 1965-66 disturbed her. I wanted so much to comfort her.

Another source of acute anxiety to me was Khushwant's language development. By the time he was four years old, his bilingual vocabulary had almost completely changed to monolingual, that is, to English. Back home in India, bilingualism was a natural course of events. Surrounded by the members of his extended family, a child experienced a rich social interaction both in Hindi and Urdu, English being added later at school. Those who have studied the history of the educational system of India appreciate its brilliance. In fact, the modern Indo-Aryan languages from the north of India, Punjabi, Hindi and Urdu, spring from the same stock as almost all European languages, including English.

This trilingual situation was a very natural one for us in the north. In fact, all over India, anyone who has had some form of secondary education would have English as their second language. It was therefore natural, I suppose, to aspire for my son to be bilingual. Our isolated situation was a hindrance in this direction. There were no Indian playmates with whom he could exchange and practise the mother tongue vocabulary. Our mutual conversation was bilingual for a while, but gradually he started to answer in English only. In later years, only when I trained to teach English as a second language, was I able to appreciate the complexities involved in learning a second language. The best I could do was to go on exposing my young son to lots of Indian culture. I had long since become disenchanted with doing so via the medium of Indian films. So while Darshan stayed at home preparing for his accountancy examination, Khush and I would pack a lunch and catch a train to London to the Commonwealth Institute. He was always enchanted by the vibrance of Indian folk and classical dancing and music.

In the field of education, Asian parents are often stereotyped as being pushy. Though it may be true in some cases, generally speaking it is simply that they place a high value on education, good manners and hospitality. Argument with adults in any context is discouraged, merely as a mark of respect. I myself was happy for Khush to argue with us at home, but circumstances under which he would have been allowed to question the judgement of his teacher were very rare indeed. Doing one's best with single-mindedness has, perhaps, a different concept for an Asian parent than for his European counterpart.

I had to strike an interesting compromise in the form of punishments for my young son. It came about after long hours of discussion with my psychology tutor at college, Dr Sanderson, a brilliant and vibrant woman whose constant encouragement helped me in countless ways. Slapping is very common in India to express disagreement or anger. I abhorred the idea. Bottom spanking to my Indian ears sounded dirty and disgusting. So we decided that a sharp smack on the legs would be a good alternative. Being the lower part of the body, it is hardly likely to produce feelings of insult or guilt. In the absence of any elders or close friends in these early years, I owe Dr Sanderson a great debt for finding time to talk me through so many confusions about my growing child. In later years, I found that removing a privilege can often be the most effective form of punishment.

In 1971, I qualified as a teacher. My first job was at Brudenell Girls' Secondary School in Amersham where I was employed as a super-numerary. (Such luxuries are rare these days.) The catchment area of this school was very select—middle to upper-middle class, and I cannot say that I experienced any real difficulties in my probationary year. After three years of such diligent study, the pay seemed ludi-crously low, but I enjoyed my job. I was glad I had pursued teaching as a career. It may have been only second best, but it had the tremen-dous advantage that my free time and holidays coincided with my son's. The school itself was not very different from the state school in New Delhi that I had attended. The girls were motivated and well-disciplined. I found teaching a very satisfying career.

In 1972, Khush and I went home for a visit. My brother Param-Jeet was refusing to set a date for his wedding unless I would promise to attend. It was impossible for me to raise the fare as I had never been allowed to have a savings account of my own. I conveyed this to my father and brother in an apologetic letter. My father made a transfer of money to my father-in-law and requested Darshan to arrange a ticket for me. Khush and I flew to India for a six-week visit in July 1972.

The prospect of seeing his grandparents and the ride in the aeroplane had excited him so much, but the change of climate hit us both very hard. Throughout our stay, Khushwant suffered from heavy nose bleeds and I had constant indigestion. There were psychological shocks too. Many typically English characteristics had become a part of my personality over the last seven years. Standing patiently in a queue, punctuality, and valuing one's privacy were three of the most obvious ones. Alas! In India, not much had changed. One could still get crushed in the undignified rush getting on to a train or a bus. Visitors arrived without prior warning and punctuality was unheard of.

We didn't really mind as both Khush and I enjoyed the colourful and noisy preparations for the much-awaited wedding of my brother. The match-maker for my brother's marriage was a favourite uncle of ours, Dr Gulhati, who was my father's best friend. We always referred to him and loved him like a real uncle. He matched the family details meticulously. Both families were army wallahs, the fathers being captains of their own units. Both the mothers were quiet, docile and very religious. Both sets of parents had taken great pains to get their children educated. Despite the system, Uncle Gulhati had made sure that both my brother and his bride-to-be, Tejinder, should meet and approve of each other. My mother visited Tejinder's household to test out her cooking skills and serving abilities. Tejinder and Param-Jeet were allowed to correspond with each other before the wedding.

The ceremony itself was a very traditional one. Everyone had been considered; everyone, that is, except the bride and the groom. The guest list reflected my father's domineering role. His relatives and friends were top priority. A lot of time was spent on what everyone else thought the bride should wear when she stepped over the threshold: all brides must look their very best and an Indian bride is no exception.

Both my mother and my father excelled in their scrupulous matching of the relatives for the *Jaimala* (garland ceremony), but no one bothered to involve my brother in his own wedding. His savings were being used to cater for most of the expenditure, yet he was not allowed to look at the guest list or comment on the type of cuisine that was to be served at his reception. No one consulted him about where the wedding ceremony should be conducted. No one wished to hear about his honeymoon plans. Our mother and father were busy making last-minute pleas for reconciliation with my uncles. After all, it had been customary to forget differences and long standing feuds on such auspicious occasions.

At this high drama of traditional dogma, I was a mere observer. Because of my past 'misdeeds', I had no rights any more. Added to this was my father's disgust over my westernised outlook on life which included my changed physical appearance, my short hair and my dress. I conformed as best I could, conducting various parts of the ceremony when required and patiently playing the part of listener for mother, brother and sisters. I kept reminding myself that I was a visitor.

Khush, meanwhile, was soaking up all the fuss that was being made of him by an adoring uncle and two doting aunts who were delighted with his winsome ways. Leaving him in their care, it was possible for me to go and relive some of my memories. I wandered about for hours through Talkatora Gardens and Buddha Jayanti Park evoking the treasured moments of the past that had haunted me throughout my married life. Nothing much had changed. Qutub Minar was still standing in all its magnificence. Our gulmohar tree was alive with blossom. The gladioli, the dahlias, the larkspurs, indeed all my favourite flowers were in bloom. The ground under my feet was familiar. I touched the branches of the gulmohar tree and leant against it. Closing my eyes I folded my hands and prayed fervently for a chance meeting with Aziz. A cold shiver ran down my spine. I could hear his voice, feel his presence; even the smell of those days was permeating through me. But he was not there. Like a ghost from the past, I walked silently along the whole length of India Gate. I visited the Mogul Gardens and the medical college. Some of the old readers and professors were still there, but no one recognised me. I wondered how many tragic tales like mine were still being written. The dream of becoming a doctor and dedicating my life to my land came flashing back once again.

The narrow high streets of Old Delhi were bustling with people bartering with the tradesmen who have developed this interchange into a fine art. The customer is always left with a false sense of gain, while the tradesman's pocket swells with profit. The beggars, the profiteers, the hoarders and the extreme corruption had stayed exactly the same for centuries. A child's voice made me stop suddenly and look back, '*Bibiji! Aapka dupatta ganda ho raha hai.*' My scarf had been dragging on the ground behind me. I patted the little girl on the head and gave her a rupee note. 'It's all right love. It doesn't matter.' I felt a stranger in my own country. I had, unconsciously, spoken to a child in English. Was I unable to express myself spontaneously in Urdu or Hindi any more? And this little Indian beggar girl, what were her future prospects? Suddenly I was frightened, restless and confused. I could no longer play any part in this medley. I felt a desperate urge to go back to England. I remembered Khush crying earlier, 'I am fed up of these flies, Mummy. Can't we go back home?' At least he knew where his home was. I had thought India was my home; I had longed to breathe its air. I realised that when a married daughter returned home, she was treated like a guest, but something else was wrong. Something was missing, not only in their treatment of me, but in my own reactions and responses. Although I tried to talk to my father, to exchange views, to give some kind of direction to my thinking, it was very painful to realise that he was never going to forgive me the past. But time and distance together had also erected barriers. I wanted to tell him about the sense of alienation and the hardships I had experienced in England. He envied me my experience of foreign lands and told me quite firmly to be grateful.

Throughout the wedding, the army band played all the popular film melodies. The wedding was beautiful. Along with his Mamaji (maternal uncle), Khushwant was enjoying being a star guest. Bhabhi Tejinder had won his heart immediately with her gently affectionate manner. He had never seen anyone dress so prettily before. Clad in a gorgeous shocking pink outfit embroidered all over in silver, she appeared to have stepped straight out of an Indian film. When the time came for us all to depart taking Bhabhi Tejinder with us, and our long blessings and cheerings were over, not many eyes were left dry.

My brother's married life had a happy start. Both parties had entered the arrangement willingly. Being our only sister-in-law, Bhabhi Teji was showered with affection and care. My sisters would not hear a word against her. My mother could never do enough for her. I did my best by sending her 'English' gifts as and when my limited means would allow. My affection was mostly expressed, however, through carefully-written letters. Alas! even she did not escape completely. While she enjoyed a lot of love and security, she too had to face my father's scorn. She was the only daughter-in-law: responsibility and blame could not be shared. The harsh conflict-ridden position of a newly-married woman has been looked at by many researchers. David Mandelbaum, an American anthropologist, sums it up thus: 'Whatever goes awry, she is apt to be called the culprit. Whenever the finger of blame is pointed, it somehow goes to her.'

Their first child, a daughter, did not arrive until 1975. On his own, my father never displayed any bias towards sons, and fully accepted it as an outcome of a natural probability. Nevertheless, there were plenty of relatives with jaundiced and opinionated views who expressed their conceited misconceptions at every available opportunity. My mother, though, has always protected her daughter-in-law most lovingly, with fierce opposition to any apportioning of blame.

On this occasion of my brother's wedding, I failed my husband yet again, as I was unable to fulfil my duty of visiting all his relatives in various parts of the country. I was happy and willing to visit my in-laws in Ferozpur, Punjab, some three hundred miles away. However, I saw no reason for tearing around the country in the heat and dust. After all, I had travelled thousands of miles to be at my brother's wedding, not to pay courtesy visits. The rains had been heavy, disrupting the rail services. I refused to oblige. Khushwant's heavy nose bleeds and loss of appetite were an added worry. Darshan ignored my explanation and wrote, 'I am looking at the post coming from my side of the relatives. You seem to have created havoc. The goodwill that your visit has earned is great. Today, I have issued four letters of apologies. You have well-above average practised your foreseen intentions of not visiting my relatives.' Not a word about the problems of a young mother and child travelling in India alone, or the lack of facilities in rural areas, or Khushwant's inability to cope with the heat. During the last week of August, my brother accompanied me for a three-day visit to the Punjab, leaving his new bride half-way through the honeymoon. Both my father and brother refused to let me go alone. From my father-in-law's house I travelled on alone to visit other relatives in the neighbouring villages. Cousin Malkeet accompanied me back to New Delhi.

For months after I returned from India, my husband's attitude towards both Khush and me remained contemptuous. I could tolerate his sardonic ridicule of me, but could not reconcile myself to his increasing rejection of his own son. He constantly cursed the day he had agreed to let me go to India. The atmosphere became stifling. Despite working full-time and contributing equally to the household finances, I was not going to be allowed to dissociate myself or diverge even slightly from the traditional role. Only in motherhood was there an escape route for self-realisation and expression. In my husband's eyes, I could have earned merit only by fulfilling the demands imposed by him and his family. It was considered my 'prime duty' to help create harmony amongst his brothers.

Letters addressed to me from my brother, sisters and parents were now censored. Every word of these letters was scrutinised and questioned, and used to support his criticism of me. My husband would often quote from the ancient Hindu epic and puranic writings to justify his behaviour towards me. A woman attains paradise, 'not by virtue of any austere penance but as a result of her obedience and devotion to her husband.'

We had both come to a point where we were experiencing a deep sense of reluctance to meet each other half way. 'Never forget that you were a rejected girl. I took pity on you and married you. You should always hang your head in shame.' My argument that a part of my life which existed before our marriage was no concern of his would only bring more demonstration of his disapproval.

About this time a remarkable coincidence occurred. Darshan, Khush and I had gone to London Airport to see off some family friends who were going to India. As the crowd of relatives started the long round of goodbye handshakes and embraces, I slipped away quietly with Khush for a short stroll.

As I walked past the information desk I bumped into someone. I had said sorry and taken a few steps, when suddenly I wanted to look back. My heart beat quickened so much it hurt. Was that Aziz? I took a few more steps. I held Khush really close and leant against one of the counters. If I were to turn round, I might be able to see him from there without letting him see me. I turned very slowly, holding onto the rails of the counter, letting them take the weight of my body.

Time stood still. It was Aziz. His gaze was fixed on me. The people, the airport building, everything disappeared from my vision. I wanted to run to him, but I could not lift my feet. There was a woman standing next to him, clad in a gorgeous sari and laden with gold ornaments; she was talking to the officials at the counter. Was that his wife? There was a little girl in his arms who could have been his daughter. Was he married, then?

I can't remember how long we simply stared at each other. Then the woman turned, started to talk to him and the three of them moved away.

'Mummy! You said I could have a sweet.' Khushwant's gentle voice seemed to come from a hundred miles away, bringing me back to life.

'Why don't you answer Khush?' Darshan was shaking me by the shoulders. 'Have you seen a ghost?' he demanded.

For months after I felt hopelessly lost, restless and disturbed. I used to imagine that if I were to go back to the airport, somehow, by the magical attraction of my love, he would be there. Had he come to England for a visit? Or did he live and practise here? I did not know.

There was also now another failing that went against me with Darshan. I had suffered from asthma for some years, but the condition was not becoming stable by the use of ordinary inhalers, and the doctor had prescribed an injection every fourth day. My mother-in-law wrote to my husband: 'My poor son, my heart goes out to you. I had not realised that we had tied your knot to a '*beemar ladki*' (sick girl). The fact that Darshan had been a diabetic since before our marriage was conveniently forgotten.

By all accounts, in the eyes of Darshan's family and friends, he was an ideal human being. From his relatives came letters full of gratitude for the lovely gifts and money that he had sent. How the whole village of Giddarbaha was envious of his sisters who had such a kind and caring older brother. Every so often, there would be complaints about each other, complaints that he had favoured one brother more than the others, complaints from his uncles that he had forgotten his 'poor relatives back home'. When he sent them money, he was thought of as a good and noble man who was assured a place in heaven by their blessings.

Living in two rooms, remembering that there was more room in my father's servant quarters, giving extra tuition to provide for the very basic necessity of food, my belief in the traditional values had been eroded away. I would not ever want to give up the tradition of looking after one's elderly parents. Only, in the case of the eldest son, 'the looking after' seems to embrace all and sundry except his wife and children. Khush and I were gradually drifting away from him. Only very occasionally would Darshan meet Khushwant's demands to play football, to go swimming and bike riding. Khushwant was at first school by then. I wanted to do everything in my job correctly and make a good impression for the sake of future references. I would look forward to spending weekends at home, and I had neither the interest nor the inclination to continue our visits to Darshan's brother in Slough.

The situation was made even worse when my sister-in-law Satwant appeared on my doorstep, with her two young sons. She had run away from home. Her parents had died when she was very young; her grand-parents had thanked providence for such a heaven-sent match as Hardev who did not embarrass and pressurise them for dowry. The fact that he was a gambler, a drunk, and had no job prospects, besides being grossly overweight, were overlooked. No doubt he would settle once he was married. Hardev used to beat his wife regularly and fairly violently. She wanted a legal separation or an injunction, and had asked for our help to resolve these matters as she did not speak any English. Darshan was adamant that she should go home. I felt trapped. I complied with her request to help translate conversations with the police, the social worker and her solicitor. I could not have just thrown out a mother with two young children to more beatings and quarrels. Both Darshan and Hardev continued to blame Satwant.

The situation was getting very tense. While I was at school, mother and sons locked themselves in. Every so often, Hardev made hoax tele-phone calls to frighten his wife. Satwant had taken the first step of leaving home without much thought. She was now sceptical and wavering. She was feeling quite frightened and did not know if she could cope with cutting herself off from all her relatives. I sympathised with her fear about resolving the economics of the situation.

And then, one day, a whole delegation of male relatives came. '*Tooney besharmy ki hud kar di*', 'You have crossed the limits of shamelessness'. '*Tooney maan baap ki izzat mitty mein daal di*', 'You have brought our honour down.' They were shouting and talking all at once. I could hear Satwant trying to defend herself, telling them about the shortage of money, and the constant beatings she received from Hardev, but it was not my place to express an opinion. If I had done so, my husband wouldn't have stopped to think twice before hitting out at me.

The relatives promised Satwant that they would keep an eye on Hardev, and they all went away, taking her with them. Before they left, I was told that it was I who had encouraged Satwant, and that, as the oldest daughter-in-law, I should have known better.

There was silence between the two families for a couple of months. Then the high drama of arguments on the telephone and visits started once again. By now, I had taken an assertive stand. Despite constant bullying and mild physical abuse, I refused to accompany my husband to Slough. I shall never forget Darshan's face as he walked through the door one midnight. A grown man, crying with anguish, with swollen eyes, the sides of his face scratched, and his nose bleeding. Apparently, he had walked into a beating session at his brother's house. Hardev had beaten Deepa, his third son, with a hockey stick, causing a hairline fracture of the skull. Darshan's interference had accelerated the tempo of an already explosive situation, and the boy had to be rushed to hospital. Hardev was dead drunk. As Darshan tried to save his sister-in-law, Hardev had hit him quite blindly, managing to pull a tuft of hair from Darshan's head.

I yelled and screamed as I tried to bring the swelling down with ice-packs.

'What do you care *maan-chod*?' (This is an extremely rude insult which casts aspersions on a woman's mother.) 'If you cared, you wouldn't have let me go alone,' he bellowed at me.

'Why do you have to go at all? You should let them sort out their own affairs. It's their business, not ours. Haven't you done your duty —many times over?'

Poor Khush! He was hiding under the bed covers, trying to shut out another of my loud bilingual outbursts.

'All our conversations, all of our quarrels, are either about money or your relatives. We never talk about us or Khushwant's future.'

'You have become too bloody English! You are unable to see that Khush is an important part of my family. What will you do when Khush is of marriageable age? You will need my relatives then.'

As usual, our argument was going off at a tangent. No amount of physical injury, insults or harassment would deter my husband from playing the role of the big brother. What about his role as a father? His role as a husband? What a joke my own role in this shambles of a marriage had become. If I tried to help, it was the wrong kind of help. If I tried to create peace, my actions were considered a threat. And if I did not intervene, I somehow became a hindrance.

What if I were to run away? I could have got an injunction on the basis of unreasonable behaviour. No—a loud voice vibrated in every single cell of my brain, boiling with indignation. I would never let my marriage become one of the many shattered statistics. Such apoplectic emotions would have to be crushed. Khushwant's childhood would be only half a childhood without a father, mere physical presence as he may have been. Yes I cared, deeply and passionately, despite feeling embittered and enraged by my husband's misplaced loyalties.

Darshan had come to understand at least one important aspect of my nature. Despite his wrenching of my arms, or digging elbows into my ribs, I would not let Khush be beaten like his cousins in Slough. I would get in the way, hit back, remove Khush from the scene, but would not allow any kind of serious physical injury to our son.

As Khush grew older, their confrontations became very brief and snappy. If ever I had to leave Khush with Darshan on his own, I would come back to tales of non-cooperation with each other. Though at the time I felt guilty siding with Khush, it was no more than Darshan's defence of his relatives. Time and time again, I searched my soul in an attempt to restore peace within that forced misalliance of a marriage. I had pleaded in tears. I had given up the housework for days to try and get my husband's attention. Occasionally, a few china cups would fall victim to my frenzied rage. But my glowering, sulphurous displays hurt only me and Khush.

And then success came for Darshan in the form of passing his accountancy examination. His whole outlook on life seemed to change. When the results came, he treated us all to a delightful Indian meal in a newly opened restaurant in Chalfont St Peter. While we both chose delicacies from a vegetarian cuisine, Khush stuffed himself with his favourite tandoori chicken and tikka. We were simply ecstatic. There was a real chance of my husband qualifying as an accountant; the prospect of that excited us both. The peace and tranquillity of those days was immeasurable.

Over the next few months, Darshan cut down his visits to Slough to a minimum. He spent every spare moment studying. Khush and I would pack ourselves a picnic and spend the day at Burnham Beeches with friends or visit the museums in London with Annabel Curry. Though my husband did not succeed with various job applications for an assistant accountant, by July 1975 he had cleared Part III of the Institute of Cost and Management Accountants exams. There were two more parts to clear. It would not have been possible for Darshan to complete this course unless he could study full-time. Together, we sat and did some detailed calculations and concluded that, so long as Darshan did not send any excessive money orders home, I earned enough to support the three of us. It was only a matter of two years. Surely, a man had a right to spend some of his life improving his prospects. All three of his younger brothers in India were now earning. They would have to support their parents between them. They all lived rent free and used the services of their mother and aunt.

Darshan applied and got a very reasonable grant to go to Hendon Polytechnic in London. He was very lucky to have got a grant as the format and the structure of the course had changed. ICMA had got the Royal Charter, aspiring to be parallel in reputation to Chartered Accountants. For a couple of years they allowed exemptions from certain subjects based on the level of passes under the old system. During the same year, I applied and got a position as a teacher at Radcliffe School, Wolverton in Milton Keynes. We would get assistance with accommodation. Milton Keynes was said to be a brand new city with a bright new future, full of anticipated prospects. We had lived in a flat for seven years. Now Khushwant would be able to have his very own room, and I would have a proper kitchen and a proper garden.

A new house, a new job and my husband's improved chances which would inevitably result from his studying. There could not have been a more promising turn of events.

11
Shared Responsibilities?

The house at Galley Hill, Milton Keynes was our first real opportunity to have a house of our very own. There was a proper kitchen and a bathroom and Khush did not have to share a bedroom with us. We even managed to buy a second-hand car.

Having finished his studies, Darshan had enrolled with the Professional Executive Recruitment to help him find a suitable job. He wrote about 150 letters to various firms up and down the country. After a stream of regrets, came the first offer—from Boots in Nottingham. Bitterly disappointed, but afraid of being left unemployed as more regret letters poured in, Darshan accepted the Nottingham post. Khush and I missed him during the week. He kept applying elsewhere, as we all considered the Boots job as only an interim measure, and within a few months, he was offered the job of an assistant accountant with a London-based clothes firm. They were due to move into their new warehouse in Milton Keynes very shortly. The new city's attractive expansion plans had found many new customers.

Thus, both our jobs were very conveniently placed. At Radcliffe School, I was promoted and given special responsibility for a general studies subject, personal relationships, for senior girls. Keith Harvey, the head of the department, had become a family friend. When the corporation made an offer which meant that we could buy our house at a discount price, it was Keith who helped us by lending us the deposit. It was like a dream come true. There was peace between us.

It may have been small by other people's standards, but after the flat at Chalfont Common, our house was like a palace to me. I planted a clematis by the front door. The soil was good and it increased in size and blossomed in such abundance that friends and neighbours introduced the expression 'green fingers' into my vocabulary.

We both felt comfortable and settled enough to contemplate having another child. Soon Khush would be eight. Life was a little sad and lonely for him sometimes. There was always the good old argument that a new baby might put new life into our own somewhat stale relationship. Darshan and I worked out our finances in great detail. This time I did not want to leave my child with a child-minder. We came to the conclusion that, if we restricted our expenditure to our planned budget, it would be possible for me to stop working for a few years. We had a few hundred pounds in savings, and for the first time we did not owe anybody any money. In February 1975 I became pregnant.

For some time, we had both felt the need to take a holiday together as a family. The invitation from Darshan's friend Dev could not have come at a more timely moment. Dev lived in Switzerland with his Swiss-German wife and a young son. Darshan had not seen Dev for nearly ten years, although back home in India they had been very close friends as teenagers.

In August 1975, we went to Switzerland by ferry and train. Both Khush and I felt mesmerised by the rich scenic splendour of the Swiss landscape. All day long, Darshan and Dev talked about some business deals that Dev was about to embark upon. Though I had heard Darshan politely refuse offers of partnership from Dev, nevertheless I felt uneasy and alarmed by Dev's constant persuasion, and heaved a sigh of relief when we boarded our train back to England.

Arune-Preet was born in October 1975. Born a Libran, one who is supposed to hate even minor disturbances around him, my young son took our household by storm from the day that he arrived. He was born with pyloric stenosis (a very tight stomach valve) and vomited constantly. He had to be fed for five minutes on each breast every half hour or so. This went on for about four months during which the time between feeds was increased very gradually. Darshan was very supportive. His attitude had become very cooperative. He would get up at night to look after Arune. He would take Khush swimming and we did not even discuss his relatives in Slough any more.

We talked often now about the future of the children. Khushwant had shown considerable promise in the direction of music. He had gained high marks in an aptitude test for music at school and was encouraged by the music teacher, Mr De Lima, to take up the violin. At the age of nine he also joined the Stantonbury Music Centre, playing in the beginners' strings and orchestra. Later, at the age of eleven, Khush auditioned and won a county scholarship. Hope and grace seemed to have found a way out of Pandora's box to shine and gleam around my life at last.

For a while, Khush, Darshan and I became totally involved in our new arrival. His enchanting ways had a captive and committed audience in us. Khush was discovering the joy and the responsibility of having a little brother. The intensity of their involvement with each other is hard to describe. At the tender age of nine, Khush was still a child in many ways. Yet he played the role of big brother with relentless cheerfulness. For me, watching them in constant communication with each other produced feelings of elation tinged with sadness. Sadness, because I found it very difficult to get away from the thoughts of India, of grandparents for the children, of festive family occasions, and of the very special position sons would have in an extended family.

Quite naturally, the bond between the three of us grew unusually strong. The only two years that I spent full-time in my favourite occupation, motherhood, were when Arune was a baby. Together, Khush and I spent many happy hours, just walking by the river in Stony Stratford, pushing Arune in his pram, or flying kites while he babbled at us from his pushchair. As soon as he was able to sit up he was strapped in the child seat on my bicycle and together we went for long bike rides and picnics.

I enjoyed telling them stories as much as they both enjoyed listening. One of my most amusing memories is of coaxing Arune into eating his supper. Together Khush and I would fabricate stories of dark and silver clouds. Arune was always the hero and of course the winner. We would pretend that our stairs were an escalator going higher and higher, up into the dark clouds. Khush and I would put on our suits of armour to save our Arune who had been captured by the dark clouds. We would cut our way through this dark labyrinth, occupied by demons, with our shining swords. Sometimes Khush would get hurt, but always we were victorious. And then by the magic of the silver clouds, we would land into the Legoworld, where we would spend hundreds of happy hours playing with computerised Lego models. And so it would go on, until Arune's sticky jammy fingers had worked through all his hair and mine, and we would all end up in the bath.

Their noise was not always music to my ears. As they grew older, brotherly love came to be demonstrated more in argument than in mere discussion. But certainly, as young children, their companionship would lift my spirits from any depth of misery.

I was beginning to feel quite secure and certain that Darshan was not thinking about business plans any more. I supplemented our income by giving tuition at home while I registered at the same time as a child-minder. I looked after two little girls and made enough money to enable me to stay at home. I was determined to look after Arune myself until he started first school. Healthwise, too, both Khush and Darshan had shown steady improvement. Khush was most definitely growing out of his asthma, which he had had since early childhood, as puberty approached; Darshan, who had hitherto dismissed my warnings about the casual handling of his diabetes, started to seek specialist advice.

And then, as if this quiet and peaceful period in my life had lasted much too long, Pandora's box opened and let out ambition, that is, my husband's ambition to succeed as a businessman. He came home one day from the office with a briefcase full of plans and ideas for a business. After putting the boys to bed, Darshan sat me down to explain his plans for starting a curios business. He must have been researching the process for setting up a company for months. I met this proposition with cold hostility. Arune was barely ten months old. We had no savings of our own. Darshan wanted to borrow two thousand pounds from our close friends. And what about the practicalities of a business? His plan was to stay at work himself and send me out to various small shops in our local high street to negotiate business. The fact that I did not drive and that the high street was a twenty-minute walk from the house was not important enough to discuss. He would himself handle market stalls on a Saturday and Sunday with Khushwant's help and together we would make a colossal success story like hundreds of Asians in this country.

For me, it was a head-on collision. I was simply not prepared to consider borrowing money from our friends. Apparently he had already approached the bank which did not see his business scheme as a viable proposition. With only one person earning, using the house as collateral was risky. Darshan criticised the bank for not being very enterprising. He had approached his relatives and they too had refused. The indignity of asking to borrow money from my best friends aside, I was not being asked how I felt. How would I cope? Somewhere in all this, the day to day chores, the time with the children, and my evening teaching, the business would have to fit. At first I pleaded and begged. 'Please, just let us wait until Arune is at least five and at school!' Then we quarrelled. A heated argument followed and for the first time in nearly two years Darshan called me those hideous, abusive Punjabi names again. He implied that I had been bad for my father in the past, and now I was determined to ruin my husband's and my family's chance for prosperity. A woman like me, a rejected daughter, should have known her place. I should have been grateful that he was consulting me at all.

'Why not start small, with one or two types of goods and with a few hundred pounds, and then build up?' I wanted to cooperate if I could. With two young children, we could not afford to take such a big risk. But there was to be no discussion. Shouting and yelling, we went into the kitchen. I did not want to ask my two best friends to lend me a thousand pounds each for a venture that could easily go wrong. I picked up a kitchen knife and handed it to Darshan. 'You don't get your way, so you call me such filthy names. Why do you hate me so much? Here is a knife. Why don't you put an end to it?' He twisted my hand to free the knife from my grip. It fell, digging into my foot and bruising a tendon. For a few days, we did not talk. Eventually, I gave up pleading under the pressure of verbal abuse and emotional blackmail and asked Annabel and Penny if they could lend us money. Penny obliged and the business was set up. If the business was successful, Darshan promised to send the children to a good public school and fulfil my ambitions for their careers in music. It was futile to revolt and refuse to cooperate. My own guilt feelings had been accentuated and brought to the surface once more. I felt that I owed it to my husband to stop arguing. As a human being he had every right to assert his personality and try out his ideas.

Later that month, Darshan went to India to form a partnership with his father and brothers. He wanted them to handle the wholesale purchase of the goods. 'Dakson Imports and Exports' was born. When he came back, he assured me that all aspects of running and forming a business had been taken care of after consultation with experts. Consignments of leather shoes, batik paintings and cotton

T-shirts began to arrive. I bought a mitre (a wooden block for cutting joints) and a framing kit and experimented to find out the best framing method for batik paintings. I quite enjoyed my new-found skill. Within a few weeks, I had sold the first batch to friends and neighbours. From five in the morning to eleven at night, we followed a carefully planned schedule, which was pinned on my kitchen wall, as we prepared ourselves for the two thousand pounds' worth of cargo to arrive soon from India. Maybe it was a good idea after all and my fears had been unfounded. I might be able to give up private tuition and evening classes and settle as a full-time business partner with my husband.

After weeks of anxious waiting the cargo finally arrived at Southampton Docks. Our order included leather goods of various descriptions, handmade inlaid wooden boxes, chess tables, and some brass objects. I could not wait to ring the authorities concerned to complete the formalities at this end. 'We are sorry Mrs Jabble, but your consignment has been somewhat damaged in a fire on board ship. If you and your husband can despatch to us all the necessary insurance papers, we can start claiming on your behalf for reimbursement.'

Surely they were joking, weren't they? What fire? Ships don't just catch fire, do they? What was the extent of the damage? The fire could not have destroyed everything—could it? In my utterly hysterical state, I did not realise the damage fire, and much more the water which is used to extinguish it, can do to wood, leather and brass. I phoned Darshan at work. For some reason he kept saying that we would go to Southampton ourselves to inspect the extent of the damage and see what could be salvaged. He kept avoiding the question about the insurance. And that was the last laugh of all in our sticky predicament. My professional accountant husband, who had tried to drill me most thoroughly in all matters concerning business, who had always made such a fuss if I had slipped in the affairs delegated to me, who had often guided other small companies in various legislative procedures, had himself simply forgotten to insure our goods. There was no insurance of any kind, so no claim could be made.

That day I behaved in a quite idiotic manner. First I locked myself in the bathroom and cried for hours. Then I took all my houseplants into the garden and made millions of cuttings. Poor Darshan. He too must have felt wretched, but showed no outward signs of dejection. I suppose that men simply do not flap or faint with fright. He rang the dock officials and asked for our goods to be forwarded to us, whatever their state.

Exactly how the packing cases had held together on their way to us was a mystery to me. The moment they were put down on the patio by the delivery man, and we tried to open one of them, it simply fell apart. Wet, smelly straw, rusty crumbling hinges, and tiny coloured bits of inlay material floated about all over the floor. Once beautiful velvet linings of trinket boxes had half an inch of mould growing on them. Brass objects such as wine glasses and candle holders were ridden with layers of copper sulphate. Somehow, some things would have to be recovered and restored to help pay the bills that amounted by then to a total of four thousand pounds. I would have to find a way. After all, I had joint responsibility for creating this mess.

In view of the hopelessness of the situation, I made urgent telephone calls to Dev in Switzerland, begging for help. I failed miserably to evoke any compassionate response in him. His attitude was one of cynical discouragement. According to him my husband had not consulted with him enough before taking such a jump in the deep end. Pleas on behalf of past friendship did not touch any nerve at all.

Our sons must have been hurt and wounded deeply to see us tear each other apart with the most wicked criticisms. Once we had exhausted all possible angles of blame and accusation, we devised yet another plan to rescue ourselves from the depths of debt. Darshan agreed to reduce the amount of money that he sent home. He got himself a weekend job with a security firm. I equipped myself with a hammer, some fine nails, varnish, odd bits of felt bought cheap, a large bottle of glue and some sandpaper, and set about recovering and repairing some of the damaged goods. It was no use being volatile about any situation in my marriage any more. I felt angry and distanced myself from everything around me.

Over the next few months, with both of us working at all kinds of odd jobs, we managed to reduce our debts by about half. I started to look for a job in earnest. I did not secretly harbour any dreams of marital bliss any more. I had never wanted to change my husband to fit in with me. I have an unyielding belief in the individuality of a person being given a chance to flourish. I had merely wanted us both to modify our thinking and personal aspirations in order to provide a suitable environment in which our sons could assert their unique individuality. For that I make no apology.

In my search for part-time jobs, I had started to look in the direction of teaching English as a second language. The BBC's most marvellous effort *Parosi* and its related neighbourhood schemes, had only just been born. And then one day I received a telephone call. It was the local co-ordinator for English as a Second Language (ESL) classes. She was asking me if I could help her to make a realistic assessment of the needs of various minority groups in the city of Milton Keynes as regards language classes. For me, it was like the dawning of a new day. Until then, my voluntary work had been limited to Girl Guides and the Junior Conservation Corps. Though I had been fully aware of the problems of bilingualism and racial stereotyping in text books, and of the dire need to promote the positive side of multi-culturalism, I had not personally had the opportunity to get involved in contributing to any of these in an effective manner. I taught on the language scheme, first as a voluntary tutor and then as a paid worker for about two years, very successfully and with enormous satisfaction. I went to Bedford College of Education two nights a week to study for the relevant RSA certificate. The following year I accepted an offer to teach biology and ESL at Wolverton College of Further Education. For me, ESL was a means to do some constructive work among people of my own kind. Through carefully planned intensive teaching, I sought to use the powerful implement of language to help my Asian sisters to bridge the gap, not only between themselves and the indigenous systems of education and employment, but also to get closer to their children.

ESL teaching had become my way to help me view my own life objectively, to see that my problems were trivial compared to many others. I came to realise the vital role Asian tutors could play in the lives of their pupils. It was very natural and appropriate for my Asian pupils to identify with me because of common links of culture and traditional patterns. Many a time, the identification became very real when we shared a common religion and language too. As a parent myself, I could share their anxieties and worries about their children. As a teacher, I was able to explain the choice of careers and the variety of jobs available.

Opportunity for some more voluntary work came my way when the

Community Relations Officer approached me to form a steering committee along with several others. The purpose was to set up a branch of the Commission for Racial Equality, later to be known as Milton Keynes Council for Racial Equality. After doing all the preliminary work, such as area profiles and drawing up of the constitution, the organisation was born in March 1978. For me, personally, there was the added delight that finally Darshan had found an activity outside the home which absorbed him completely. He was elected treasurer and he took on his role with great zeal. I stayed on the executive for a couple of years, but later found that the council was unavoidably assuming much more of a political role. I was happy to work in the background, promoting and advancing educational and cultural activities. Besides, Darshan had insisted that my place was at home in the evenings, and that he did not approve of my ever-increasing 'Englishness'.

Darshan enjoyed his executive status; he devoted all of his spare time to the financial affairs of the Council and regularly attended meetings with other officials. Inevitably, there was conflict. Khush, Arune and I were driven away from him even further by this new set of circumstances. After all, I had encouraged and nominated him for the post of treasurer. I had no right then to expect him to participate in the unimportant and trivial activities of the children. At work, too, I was awakening to a different kind of role conflict. When Khush was a baby, I was at college and had not experienced the guilt caused by divided loyalties. But now from time to time Arune would contract one of the series of common ailments children the world over have gone through since time began. If it was something minor, I would not take time off. I would leave him with the child-minder, and cycle back and forth during a free lesson and at lunch time. Occasionally, Darshan would help, but if there was an important prior engagement, I would be left to sort out the prescription and the doctor's appointment on my own.

In those days of utter naïvety, I used to think that if one had dedication enough to keep up to date with new developments, if one explored and practised good teaching methods, if one proved oneself to be dependable and reliable, one would gain promotion automatically. Since those days, I have, I hope, become a little wiser, grown up and matured to the reality. As I have heard it said so often, 'Alas, no one hands you a medal for being conscientious'. There must be thousands of working mothers like me who have to contend with this guilt, this conflict from time to time between the care of our children and attendance at work. I certainly do not know many men whose souls are tortured by this dilemma. Unfortunately, in later years this problem became even more acute as, at the age of five, Arune-Preet developed chronic asthma. Even a minor infection of the respiratory tract played havoc with his breathing and digestion. Of course, there was a positive side. He had to learn to look after himself and this made him quite independent at a very early age.

During the early part of 1979, we tried once again to arrange for my mother-in-law to come and join us. Permission was granted for her to come for a holiday for six months. She was getting old and we both thought that it would give her a nice long break, while helping us out with Arune at the same time. I was aware of the difficulties in the change of culture and language that she would encounter, but amongst my students on the language scheme were many elderly ladies who were ready to befriend her and who would help make her stay a pleasant one.

We failed to convince her of our intentions. There was now an irreconcilable status quo between her and Darshan. She refused to even consider it. Most sons from England sent ten times as much money as we had managed. In her view, we had not done right by her at all. We had no right to ask her for such favours. Though I felt angry, reluctantly I wrote her a long letter, asking for forgiveness for the past, explaining the business failure and the fact that I had not been to work while Arune was very young, but she did not consent.

My work with the Commission for Racial Equality had also opened my eyes to the overwhelming problems of young Asians caught between two cultures. So when Puneet, Darshan's nephew, approached us to become his legal guardians, I could not refuse. He had fallen out with his parents, had several convictions against him and would be sent to prison if we did not help. Puneet was settling down well, when his mother started a series of telephone calls and requests to return home. He responded to his mother's pleadings and left us half-way through his CSE examinations, failing to attend a few interviews for apprenticeship that I had applied for on his behalf. I urged Darshan to intervene. Was false pride really more valuable than a young life? Yet again I was told that I had invited this drama into my household. Therefore I alone should act in it. Puneet went home. Several misadventures followed and he was sent to prison for four years. Poor Puneet! Because of the false pride of his parents and my husband, he was denied the one chance of giving his life some sort of shape.

Khushwant's own teenage years brought their own pains and pleasures. The only two people against whom a child can assert his own personality, direct his anger and yet expect sympathy and understanding, are his parents. If one parent is non-existent either physically or simply by refusing to take an active part in this inter-personal conflict, then the other parent must automatically play the dual role. Darshan's failing health made him very self-indulgent and irritable with the children. There was a clash of interests here too: Darshan was a wrestler and a hockey player in his youth. I think he resented the fact that Khush never enjoyed sport.

The violin was his major interest. In the early days, when the concerts in which Khushwant performed were of short duration, Darshan used to come along, especially as Arune-Preet was always enthralled by seeing his big brother on stage. Sadly, though, Darshan had no patience with classical music, Indian or European. He found it all rather boring. As Khushwant's commitment became deeper and his playing more advanced, Darshan simply refused to attend. To be talented in such a fine instrument may have been a gift of the gods for some, but *Match of the Day* on the screen in the corner of our living room deserved far more attention from my husband than the three of us.

In this context the saddest occasion that I recollect was in November 1981. Khushwant had just finished a year as the leader of the Stantonbury Training Orchestra. The orchestra had been giving a series of concerts in the city. The final concert was reported in the local newspapers. 'A packed Woughton Church enjoyed a varied musical programme from the Training Orchestra of Stantonbury Music Centre. The young musicians led by Khushwant Singh Jabble began with the overture to the Pirates of Penzance . . . ' An immense source of joy to Arune and me, but my husband was at home being entertained by an international football match.

I did not achieve success in giving the boys any command of the Hindi language, though I tried to provide a variety of live situations, whereby the boys would asssimilate some cultural influences. This was a source of great disappointment to both sets of grandparents. In a town like Slough, with a large Asian community, this assimilation would have happened quite naturally. Dispersal may encourage integration, but it takes away certain important elements of one's upbringing, such as a feeling of belonging, of security. Dispersal causes isolation. Coupled with indifferent and hostile reactions from the indigenous community a child is prevented from recognising the benefit of a multi-cultural environment. A rejection of one's home culture can set in, and is often carried into adulthood.

Khush and I talked a lot about the generalised newspaper and media propaganda on India's poverty. It was neither desirable nor possible to shelter him from documentaries focusing on the poverty in the Third World. Yet I wanted him to be proud of his Indian-ness. I could not recreate for Khush and Arune any of the many splendid places and views of India, the vast openness of the wheat fields of the Punjab, the giant mango groves, or the magical ecstasy of sleeping under the stars. But I could and did try to expose my young sons to Indian literature. I could only hope that, with my sympathy and love, Khush would not let the hostility induce negative feelings in him. He had some anxiety about his colour in those early days and did not react kindly to patronising, 'one of us' attitudes. I suppose that this was a trait he acquired from me. I had trained as a teacher in this country and could never see myself as anything other than an individual as good as anyone else. But for most of my colleagues, I was always an Indian and an immigrant first, a teacher and a human being second. Successful integration did not mean mutual understanding, but compromising with the English point of view. As long as my opinion on any subject was not a deviation from the known variations on the theme, it was acceptable. Otherwise, one would have to stand alone. I had to learn about being a woman in my own right in a society where the stereotype of an Indian woman is the passive wife with her head covered, her hands folded and her eyes cast down, walking three paces behind her husband.

And so we muddled through Khushwant's juvenile years. Our opposing viewpoints sometimes clashed, but always we tried to compromise. There was little or no room for sadness with Arune for company and to keep us on our toes. Generally speaking, in a western society the mother seems to act as the chief mediator between various outside agencies and the child. I had come to accept that role. Due to a particularly nasty bullying episode at his school, I had to intervene and arrange to transfer Khush to a different middle school in his last year.

Back home in India, both my sisters Inder-Jeet and Sweety had successfully finished their degrees in botany and chemistry. Marriages had been arranged for them with their consent; neither of them had dared to entertain the idea of a love marriage. I can only guess that my embittered saga must have served as a good example to incite all my sisters and cousins to uphold *izzat* for all time to come. During their pubescent years, I had to repress the temptation to express my views on the subject. I knew that my father censored my letters, always, before allowing my mother and sisters to read them. There was no point in writing about my own life's trials and tribulations. I had to be, and act, a little aloof. I missed them so terribly though.

I regularly used to send them all, even Darshan's brothers and sisters, gifts for birthdays and festive occasions. That was in the hope of keeping a link going for the sake of a feeling of belonging, of continuity for the children. Though I was too far away to be consulted on any major issues, my mother did write to me once about finding a match for Sweety. But, knowing my views on the orthodox arrangement, my father stopped me from doing any negotiations when the actual time came. That a sister of mine might come to live here was an ephemeral dream that had evaporated for ever. Gradually, I was beginning to realise the separateness of my existence from the rest of them. Inside me there was always a constant struggle between my heart's desire and my actual situation. Most of the time I managed to humble and sober myself by lending a sympathetic ear to other people's melancholy stories. There were times, though, when nothing helped to calm the overwhelming wish to be with my family in India.

My sisters did not continue the frank exchange of views that existed between us before their marriages. My brother Param-Jeet had become preoccupied with his own family and career. From time to time, though, there was a sensitive concern expressed in my sister Inder-Jeet's letters.

There seems to be a familiar and uniform pattern that exists everywhere in the world known as 'a woman's lot', whether you be from the East or the West. Perhaps I had always been too much of an individual to simply sit back and accept it as mine. Trapped in a marriage where virtually all my feelings had been dictated by tradition, the essence of my whole being was wrapped up in creating a measure of peace in that situation. And yet there had been 'love' in the past. The resultant feelings and associations had hindered my attempts at peaceful co-existence with Darshan. If that co-habitation had failed, nothing else would have been open to me. So I had to go on trying, pretending that nothing much was wrong, that it would be all right one day. Yet I fe't I needed help. I felt suffocated. I could not respond to my husband in physical terms, no matter what futile ways and means I employed. It came to be the worst nightmare of my life. The issue could not be discussed with outside agencies. One could confer with relatives, but the discussion would be limited to ways and means of reconciliation only. This was acceptable to Darshan, but not to me. I would have sought counsel from a marriage guidance clinic, but my pride, my ego would not allow me to lay myself open to criticism by my husband's relatives.

Something else had started to go wrong. Darshan had developed oedema (water retention) in his legs. He refused to accept this as a warning, perhaps of kidney malfunction, and generally ignored the doctor's advice to lose weight. He insisted that there was no danger of his present condition ever becoming a threat. Whenever I wanted to talk about it, he would criticise my cooking and lay the blame for his illness on me. He would bring up the past and tell me to mind my own business.

In March 1979, Darshan was taken to hospital in an emergency. He had come home from work feeling cold and sweating. We both thought that he had flu, but in the morning, when I took him his early morning cup of tea, he was quite stiff. Dr Chambers came and tried to wake him, but failed. Darshan had been in his first hypoglycaemic coma for fourteen hours.

Alas! Darshan failed to recognise the consequence of his casual approach to what was now a very complicated prognosis. '*Marna hai to khaatey, peetay maro*?' 'If you are going to die anyway, why not enjoy your food at least?' was the philosophy he used to justify his passion for food.

12

When Mother Came

'Most mothers play a very passive, a very submissive role', so the
experts in sociology would have us believe about Indian women. If I
was asked to single out one person whose life most influenced the
shaping of my personality, it would be my mother. Passive and submissive she may have been, but a staunch and stern personality who
never lost her radiant dignity and self-respect for a moment, certainly
never in public. We were a joint, an extended family. Grandpa had
died before I was even born. Babuji assumed the role of the 'father
figure'. I believe that he enjoyed the autocratic authority that this
position brought him. I believe too that he revelled in self-admiration,
a kind of extreme egotism. I often heard him telling my uncles how
they would never have been educated if it had not been for him. This
attitude was to part him later from brothers and sisters, though he had
truly spent many years of tension and financial struggle getting them
educated and finding suitable partners for them. My mother's role was
clearly dictated by a mixture of circumstances and traditions. In a pat-
riarchal structure, she had the assumed role of *bari bahu* (most senior
daughter-in-law). At weddings, funerals and other ceremonial occasions, of which there were always many, she was expected to give and
give. Give, that is, her services as a hostess, and presents, at the expense
of sacrificing what by right of birth belonged to my brother and me.

One episode will always remind me of how she tried to inculcate
these qualities into me. A cousin of mine was getting married. My
father had bought her a beautiful Punjabi silk suit as a present. As the
uncles exchanged gifts during the ceremony, my cousin's father said
to my mother, 'Bhabhiji! It is not enough to have provided just a suit,
you really should have had a gold ornament made too.'

Mother took it quite seriously, came over to me, took my gold ring off my finger and gave it to my cousin, saying, 'Jeet was only wearing it for safe-keeping.'

In all my teenage years that ring was my only ornament, a prized possession, an award for my outstanding performance at school. It was never replaced.

My mother played a role of subservience and total obedience to my father. She would not even have dreamt of rebelling against him. This would have meant dishonouring her parents. All her gentleness and patience did not alter my father's behaviour towards her a fraction. She suffered his oppression in silence. She came from a relatively poor family, with six younger sisters. Time and again my father secured a match for each of the sisters. For this, my mother and grandmother displayed their gratitude to my father and suffered his insults in silence. Mother was totally dependent upon my father financially, though I always felt strongly that she was giving enough service in return for her economic dependence. My father always had the last word in all decisions. In addition to the care of his two younger brothers and sister, he had to arrange a second marriage for his older sister, because she became a widow very early on. This caused considerable hardship to my parents as arranged marriages involve a lot of gift giving in the form of a dowry. For a widow, the cost could easily be double. My father was much too stubborn to ask his older brother for help. Instead, to help out financially, mother started to sew clothes for other people, working all hours of the night. This meant increased responsibility for me, looking after my brother and two young sisters.

Through all this struggle she always felt that she would never have suffered if she had had a brother. In India, the relationship between a brother and a sister is egalitarian. In my case it was intensely so. Mother continually reminded me of my good fortune in being blessed with a brother, as she herself was so very unfortunate and doomed. Rakshabandhan was the festival at which a sister ties a coloured thread on her brother's wrist and he gives her a gift and pledges to protect her all her life. It was ritually celebrated with great reverence every year.

Though my brother had been promoted to the rank of a major, my father always labelled him a failure. As the years rolled on, my father's attitude to my brother and his own brothers approached a state of near tyranny. Though my brother could not break loose, my uncles went their separate ways despite my father's disapproval. They refused to accept his absolute authority, particularly in decisions affecting their lives. Mother always supported him in public, though she shed countless tears in private. She was always the object of ridicule. By some peculiar twist, most of the relatives managed to blame her for my father's display of indifference, particularly his lack of show on ceremonial occasions. He refused to be drawn into competition as regards gifts and entertainment. For this I admired him, at the same time resenting his refusal to socialise with his relatives. He preferred to socialise with his officer friends. Mother always felt out of place there as she was not educated and could not easily get into conversation on topics of current interest. In matters of domestic skill, such as cooking and embroidery, though, I have never met anyone more proficient.

For a while in 1980 things seemed reasonably secure financially. I had been back at full-time work some three years and had saved up enough to pay for a visit back home. Instead, the boys and I decided that it would be nice if Grandmother could come to England for a holiday. It would be a marvellous opportunity for them to get to know their grandma, to experience her love, and she could develop a close relationship with them. It was altogether a better, more practical idea. Suddenly, my mind was filled with tentative dreams of going shopping with Mother, taking long walks, going to the Neath Hill Gurudwara, maybe even have an *Akhand Path* Ceremony in our own house. Unconsciously my youth and childhood were visiting me again. After all, the intimate and confidential companionship a girl shares with her mother is unique and there can be no substitute. I was looking forward to philosophising with her on my innermost feelings of isolation and hurt. It might even be nice for Darshan to experience the care and affection of a real mother-in-law.

To this day, I can remember vividly the profound quivers and flutters in my stomach as Mother walked through the customs. Everyone around her seemed to have disappeared in a mist. There she was with the same old quiet dignity, looking more like my older sister in a traditional pale green Punjabi suit. She spotted Darshan first of all, walked quietly up to him and embraced him gently.

'Hello! *Betaji, tum theek to ho na*?' 'You are well I hope?'

Khush was waving like mad. They reached for each other and were lost for a few magic moments in each other's arms.

'*Bete! Tum kitne bare ho gaye*', 'You have grown up so! My darling child. Where's Jeet and Arune?' And then she saw us. Her tight embrace brought floods of tears. Arune clung to me tightly. 'Who was this stanger we were all making such a fuss of?' he must have thought, I suppose.

'Come on silly! Say hello to Grandma.' But he wouldn't budge.

In the days that followed, though, they grew very close and of course she became the best grandma in the world. He ate, slept, played with Grandma every day naturally, and with tremendous fondness got her involved in everything he did.

Gradually, she became aware of Darshan's indifference to the boys, and his lack of interest in our household. Over the past fourteen years I had not written to her about our incompatibility, about his total commitment to his family here and back home. She was upset over the 'make-shift' bed that I had set up for myself downstairs and the total lack of harmony between us. We lived very separate lives under the same roof. She was quite shocked to discover that he did not practise any religion, neither Sikh nor Hindu. Her opinion of the situation kept swaying, at times in my favour, at times against me. She found his verbal and physical abuse of me quite alarming.

'Jeet! Why did you never write to us about all this?'

She had forgotten how I had in the beginning written every detail, and they had never wanted to hear. It was my *kismet*, I was told. I tried not to argue with her. I wanted to make it a truly memorable holiday for her. We did lots of shopping together. The boys and I took her to Brighton, Windsor and London, and put together two photograph albums for her to take back.

For a while, Mother indulged in furious criticism of my in-laws. I was very fortunate in her eyes as I had sons and not daughters. What was I going to do about my husband? A mother of sons should have been able to command more respect. Why did I have to work all hours of the day? She could not forgive Darshan for bringing me to this country under false pretences.

One night we talked until late.

'I am quite content to be living in this country, Mother dear, and I am not alone in my predicament. You must understand that it is a very common situation in England. And tell me, exactly how do I demonstrate my unhappiness over my domestic situation. If I was to acquire his kind of apathy, where would it lead my children? Shall I get a divorce?'

'Bite your tongue!' Like lightning, her hand fell across my face.

'What do you want me to do? You don't want me to get a divorce. You don't like my situation. So what would you have me do?'

'Maybe we should send for your father.' Her suggestion sounded so absurd and comical.

'And have him turn my life upside down again, Mother! I am thirty-five years old. What do you want to do? Arrange another marriage for me? Or are you going to change my husband's habits by waving a magic wand?'

'I don't see any point to all that education you had. Your life is worse than mine. At least I have servants to do the menial chores.'

We sat until two in the morning talking and discussing. I didn't mind that she had hit me physically. The 'culture-gap', however, hurt deeply. Over the next couple of months I tried to make her realise that divorce was the only solution for me, and that I could not contemplate returning to India. To my children, England was home. I had to fight for a life for me here.

She began to see the reality of life in England. In the land of 'milk and honey' many Indian women from the villages of Punjab, Gujrat and Bengal lived in 'ghettos' oppressed and lost in the silent bewilderment they could not break through because they did not have the tools to do so. Some of the differences which affected a woman's role here were easily identifiable. She was also beginning to see the influence of hidden inhibitory forces bred into Indian women, brought up with a strong sense of duty and tradition.

I also wanted to tell her that time had not healed some other wounds. That I still cherished a memory, that as a woman I had had tremendous difficulty in responding to my husband, and that in the eyes of God and in the eyes of Indian law, I had married only one man. But I did not discuss the issue with her. There wasn't a hope of finding Aziz and what if I did find him? I did not wish to dwell on the subject too deeply. There were enough problems anyway, without creating any more.

We discussed at great length the bridal pyres still being lit in India.

She was able to narrate many hundreds of real incidents. At least I had escaped such a fate and had only suffered the verbal sarcasm of my husband and his parents. Every year, some two to three hundred young women and sometimes mothers of very young children are burnt alive or beaten to death due to acute 'gift-exchange' and dowry problems.

Mother's position was typically Indian. She did not utter a single complaint to Darshan, though there were so many questions she wanted answered. Traditionally the relationship between a mother and her son-in-law is one of mutual respect. There was no defined role for me though. It had been very difficult and tiring emotionally and physically to keep one's feet dangling in two cultures. The reality was that there was nothing to fall back on in times of crisis. I did not truly belong to either world. Financially, I contributed equally, yet I had complete responsibility for housework and the boys. Added to which was my own stubborn determination that Khush would carry on with violin lessons and other extra-curricular activities no matter what.

The actual process of divorce, at any rate, would have been simpler back home. We both could have counted on our respective parents. The nervous tension in our children would have been lessened by close relatives removing them physically from the situation. Mother was able to see, finally, that there was only one way out. She was going to go back 'home' in a few days. My 'home' was here. My expectations from my children, my concept of happiness and my hopes for old age were all very different from hers. She was beginning to understand that struggling alone in my isolated circumstances had changed my personality. I looked only to myself for hope and help. It troubled her deeply that Darshan had exploited my services to the full and that there was nothing she could recognise as being his duty. She felt embarassed by his constant harassment of me, his constant fault-finding with my cooking.

'You should have at least taught her to cook before tying this useless burden to me!'

Poor Mother! She had to hear this about a daughter whose cooking had often won praise, and keep silent.

She was shocked to discover that he was a diabetic. She was disturbed further by the lack of control Darshan exercised in his eating habits. She held my hands and cried at their roughness. She took photographs of every chore I did, like putting up a fence, fixing guttering to the greenhouse, gardening, turfing and painting, while my dear husband simply slept.

'Really, Mother, you should be proud of me. Think of millions of *majdoor* women (labourers) in India, proudly building bridges and canals,' I tried to reassure her.

'But you were not born into a *majdoor* family. You are the daughter of an army officer. We thought we were marrying you to a respectable, educated God-fearing man. You live like a down-trodden slave in his house. You don't even have a washing machine. You cycle everywhere.'

I felt very angry that I had been exposed in this manner to my own mother. I had invited her for a well-deserved, well-earned holiday. I tried to make her understand that Khush and Arune were my precious reasons for struggling on with life. They were my adornments, my *izzat*. That was what I lived for, to help them grow into two fine, independent and decent human beings. Wasn't she proud of them?

'The boys and I have each other's love and complete trust. There aren't many who could say that. There will be some solution. Don't feel sorry for me because I go teaching on a bike in the evening, in snow, storms or rain. Why don't you think positive? I have at least a job to go to.'

'Let's write to your uncle in Dubai, Jeet! Please let me do something. Uncle Pritam owes me a favour. I have only got to ask.'

Her outrageously emotional display unnerved me and I started to wish she had never come.

'Please remember, Mother! You are here for a short stay. I have seen you twice in fourteen years and will probably not see you again for another fourteen. You can't do anything about my situation. I have to do right by my sons and myself.'

She could see signs of rebellion in her *pativarta* daughter (one who worships her husband as God). Mother expected and assumed me to be *pativarta*; she knew that I was torn between traditions from back home and life's continual challenges. She could see how the struggles and tensions of a marriage that never was had produced a desire for emancipation in me. I had always seen my wedding ceremony and subsequent married life as a funeral march.

'Have you ever known anyone live through their own funeral

march?' I did not want to hurt her and yet, in her presence, a kind of self-pity, self-indulgence had taken me over.

'Remember your joy over a "foreign-returned" son-in-law?,' I reminded her wryly. Like a kite with its string cut, my being, my body, my soul was caught in the web of life. I had no claim to mother's affection and attention any more. Her vision of me, lavished with gorgeous gold ornaments and leading a luxurious life in England, had been shattered. She was embarrassed by the extremely adverse circumstances in which she had found her beloved daughter. She was so distressed and disappointed at the mediocrity of her son-in-law, at his materialistic tendencies to the exclusion of all else.

'When I get back, I am going to tell your father. I promise you he will sort something out.' Perhaps she had at last accepted that my marriage had come to an end. *'Yeh kaisa hai? Ise to izzat se bolna bhi nahin aata.'* 'What kind of a man is this? He does not speak to even me, his mother-in-law, with respect.'

I wanted to tell her about my loneliness in marriage, about my yearning to be loved, to be cared for. But it would have only created more anguish for her. Besides, this was no time for self-pity. I would care for myself and find strength. I was lucky to enjoy good health. The strict discipline of keeping up a fitness routine and a sensible diet had paid dividends. I was not going to accept my life as a *fait accompli*. She was pleased with my firm belief in prayer. From time to time a Sikh would endeavour to read the whole of the holy book. In *Khulla Path* (open prayer), there is no time limit, and the completion of the reading is celebrated by giving a 'community meal'. We did *Khulla Path* in the month that followed.

Arune-Preet's memories of those days must be so special. He spent every moment with her that he could. She walked him to the nursery and waited eagerly to collect him at lunchtime. It was a very warm and touching experience to watch them communicate. Mother spoke hardly any English. Arune-Preet knew only the very basic words of Punjabi. Yet together they developed that most special language of all, the language of lovt. Their sign-language for each other was perfected to a fine art. They played ball games and flew kites.

During Mother's stay with me, two episodes occurred which must have disturbed her, but also gave her an insight into the racial tension which prevails in degrees all over England. For a whole week there were eggs thrown at our windows every night, and then one morning we woke up to discover to our horror that 'Pakis Go Home' was painted all over the garden fence on the outside in white paint. Every now and then, racism raises its ugly head in one form or another. It is an inexplicable phenomenon. We not only have to learn to live with it, we have to try hard as parents to minimise its effects on our children's attitudes. In Indian people I have noticed an incredible tolerance to any amount of racial attacks. We tend not to be demonstrative, though we find such behaviour quite obscene.

The second episode was connected with the school where I was teaching at the time. A couple of fifth-formers made some thoroughly obnoxious telephone calls to my house. They had managed to steal the staff telephone list from the office. Fortunately, Khushwant had a day off school due to an asthma attack the previous night, and he was at home.

'Mrs Jabble has had a car crash and has been taken to Stoke Mandeville hospital. We are sending a taxi round to your house. You should come immediately.'

Both my mother and my son were badly shaken. Khushwant had the common sense to ring the school and I was able to calm them both down. I hate to think how Mother would have reacted had she been on her own. She would have picked up the words 'accident' and 'hospital' and would have got into the taxi in utter confusion. The police were informed and thanks to a housemaster who recognised the tactics of one of the boys, they were quickly caught. As no one was physically hurt, the boys were simply cautioned and fined. I did not remonstrate in any way as there was nothing that could have been done. I thought of asking for a written apology from the boys, but for fear of making a fuss I did not bother.

'What is this *tamasha* (circus-show)?' '*Yeh gore aapne mulak mein 200 saal rahe*', 'These white people lived in India for two hundred years.'

'No, Mother darling! They did not just live in India. They *ruled* India for two hundred years.'

'No matter, your father worked alongside white people more than half his life.' She paused. 'Does this sort of thing happen all the time?'

The humiliation of racist abuse was something that I had come to live with almost every day of my life. Though I had learnt to face a racist with cold, calculated indifference, it was not always easy. I felt an intolerable disgust at being called a fucking Paki bastard or a black wog, and hearing racist jokes. Oh yes! Jokes about Cambodians, Pakis, blacks and currently Ethiopians, made me want to throw up. I could even learn to be tolerant to these comments, mostly made by young adolescents. But it was the adults I feared most, those adults who loved to bait me, and then make a meal of my sensitivity. My response to English cynicism was often also incorrect, as an Indian person of my generation will do her utmost to remain polite for fear of giving offence.

Besides, I did not know how to deal with racist comments about my culture from my colleagues. For fear of losing my job, I would say nothing. No matter what quality of excellence I achieved in my classroom teaching and discipline, lack of higher degree qualifications had been given as a reason for my not being promoted. My involvement with developing community languages and ethnic arts festivals around the city was never supported by my white colleagues. However, some of the children attended some of the performances and even took part in some of the workshops. I was once told that I was giving such a lot of time to my community commitments, I could not be doing my job well. This was after a dramatic confrontation with a colleague who had refused to co-operate with me during an inspector's visit. From then on, I always taught with the door of my classroom open, an open invitation to anyone, any time who cared to check on my teaching.

Poor Mother though! I am sure she was thoroughly perplexed by the whole episode. She took back with her like most visitors a mixture of feelings about England and the English, together with a growing fondness for her grandsons.

13
Comex-10, 1980

The events of 1980 brought a renewed determination in me to save my marriage at all costs. By the beginning of 1980, when Darshan started to suffer from oedema, he was on eight different drugs including insulin, and a strict diabetic diet. Being a vegetarian he consumed large quantities of vegetables. Some of these, like potatoes, had to be leeched by boiling to get rid of certain minerals. He was warned that unless he observed the diet restrictions he would damage his already malfunctioning kidneys irretrievably.

In June 1980, while my mother was still with us, Darshan received a letter from his mother. She was supposedly facing imminent death and wanted Darshan to go immediately. (She is still alive today.) Despite the advice of the renal specialist at Churchill Hospital that to go in mid-summer could prove to be fatal, Darshan left for India in July. He had intended to go for four weeks, but after two weeks, I received a telegram. He was returning home, suffering from dysentery and enteritis. As he walked through our front door, his dehydrated body gave way. He had lost about two stone. I helped him change and wash, called the doctor and prepared his special meal for him. Darshan pushed the meal away and told me to prepare proper food.

'What about the diabetic diet?' I asked.

'To hell with the diet! I nearly died out there and you have to go on about the diet!' he shrieked. I watched quietly. During the following few days he had me prepare lavish, spicy Indian dishes. The illogicality of his own actions was lost on him. I kept my silence, for fear of abuse, though desperately wanting him to stop and see the folly of his ways.

Temporarily, his health seemed to improve and he returned to

work. But in August he landed in hospital in an emergency. He had had total renal failure.

'They are going to put me on peritoneal dialysis.'

This is dialysis across the peritoneum, conducted through a catheter tube attached to the front of the abdomen. The dialysis bag can be carried folded in the trouser pocket. He sounded so frightened. I reassured him as best I could, trying to take in the complexity of his condition. Dr Oliver, the specialist at the Churchill Hospital, talked to us both together. Darshan would need a separate room and I was not to handle any of his equipment as the risk of infection of the peritoneum was high. He would have to go through the strict routine of changing the fluid bags four times a day by himself. He was told that he must carry on working full-time to avoid any psychological effects of the treatment. His employers at Hoechst UK were very sympathetic and helpful. For the mid-day change he could either come home or use the facilities provided at work.

I assured him that I would help him in every way. If his illness brought *rapprochement* in our lives, then I would let bygones be buried. I laid down two strict conditions though, not to be broken on any account. He would have to stop every kind of physical and verbal abuse of me. He must put an end to his deep involvement with his relatives and start taking a proper interest in the daily lives of the boys. He owed it to himself to remain at peace with his family. The time for playing the big brother role was now over. He must realise that our generosity had been overstretched as far as his relatives were concerned. We could save our marriage and his life with single-minded devotion. I said that we had come to live in this country, and we couldn't keep all of our own culture. I begged him to take his health seriously. The cultural traits which were needed in the past to satisfy his ego would have to be forgotten now. His health must be top priority. If it was possible, we would move to a bigger house.

So we set out to shape our lives around my husband's worsening condition with a good deal of optimism. Khushwant and Arune-Preet were moved into one bedroom. Together the boys and I prepared a room for Darshan. We painted it, changed the furnishings and bought a brand new orthopaedic bed. On one of our visits to the hospital the renal specialist explained the kidney problems of their father and the importance of observing clinical hygiene to Khush and Arune. From then on, they were both as helpful as the limitations of being children would allow. I started to look for contacts with other families in a similar situation to ours. There was considerable help available. Unfortunately, despite my pleading and persuasion, Darshan refused to join either the Diabetic Support Group or the Association of Kidney Patients from whom he could have derived sustentation, both morally and socially.

We put our house on the market with a view to finding a slightly larger property nearer to Darshan's work, to cut down on his driving. We decided on Parkside, Furzton, some four miles from Hoechst, a third of the distance from Stony Stratford. The estate was within walking distance from Denbigh School and that would eliminate transport problems for me. We instructed our solicitor to start the negotiations.

As Khush grew up, it had started to become quite apparent that there was little correlation between my attitude and his with regard to his ethnocentricity. It was time to develop an awareness and understanding of his cultural conflict, rather than fight against it and let our relationship deteriorate. Up until he was about twelve it seemed natural to let him see the world through our eyes only. If ever an incident occurred where his differences in colour and kind were exaggerated and scorned, it was quite easy to comfort him by philosophising about those who pick on others being poor sorts of people with nothing better to do. I wanted him to be proud of his heritage. The cultural differences which are looked upon as 'difficulties' by eminent child psychologists are, in my view, unique and positive factors. Under the loving guidance of their parents, it is perfectly feasible that children of my son's generation should be inculcated with the best of both worlds. 'Cultural shock' comes from the fact that a teenager is learning to reconcile three major influences, the home background, his own personality, and society, which is in a continuous state of flux. Expressions of love, hate, anger and disappointment are often very different and far more open in the Indian culture than they are in a western society. One way is not necessarily better than the other. A black or Asian teenager standing at these crossroads perhaps needs additional support and trust from his parents.

Exaggerated reports of racial tension on television, and the critical analysis of 'the immigration problem' in the press, accentuated our fears about our safety. Enoch Powell, the Conservative M.P. for Wolverhampton, speaking at the annual general meeting of the West Midlands Area Conservative Centre had made his historic speech on the issue of immigration in November 1968. He warned the nation that unless immigration was reduced there would be widespread unrest as the English would not tolerate their land being turned into an alien planet. 'Like the Romans, I seem to see the river Tiber foaming with much blood.' He also demanded compulsory repatriation of Commonwealth immigrants. With such racist propaganda it was impossible to walk down the street without receiving abuse.

Despite my optimistic hopes for the future, alas, Darshan was not very tolerant of the emerging cultural pluralism. He and his friends always talked of the lack of security they felt. 'We are here to stay, even if we have to fight' was not his philosophy. They dreamed of building property in India, of never trusting the English, of going back home one day. And there I was, shielding my young son from this hatred on both sides, trying to teach him the true meaning of integration. Roy Jenkins, then Home Secretary, had said in the 1970s, 'I define integration not as a flattening process of assimilation but as equal opportunity accompanied by cultural diversity in an atmosphere of mutual tolerance.' How was I going to turn this 'cultural diversity' into an advantage rather than a handicap? The media had only too often overplayed certain situations that make a 'good story'. And though racism, unemployment and homesickness were not exactly pleasant experiences, the prospect of returning home was a pretty dismal and unrealistic one. One had to take into account the feelings and aspirations of one's children who had, as I said earlier, divided loyalties.

Darshan and his Asian friends carried on discussing discrimination in housing and employment, and continually reminiscing about the days of the Raj. Though never wishing to underplay their anxieties and feelings of insecurity, I felt that there was no need to over-expose Khush and Arune to such cheerless and disagreeable unpleasantness. I used to remove them from the scene on some pretext or other. No doubt they would become aware of the permanent backdrop of hostile racism in due course.

The hope that the boys should acquire some of the traditional Sikh customs was more or less lost. It felt very awkward always to pray on the various *gurupurabs* (commemorative days) by myself. It seemed very odd to say lengthy prayers for the recovery of my agnostic husband. I felt that it was cruel to force the boys to sit through three to four hours of preaching when they could not comprehend the language of the Granth at all. But I wondered what my father would have thought of his Hindu son-in-law who never missed a chance to scorn and mock the Sikh ceremonies.

I stopped trying to impose religious dogma or the strict traditional practices. The customs that the children enjoyed would be automatically absorbed into their personalities as they grew up. It is only possible to recreate the folklore and the festivals when there is a substantial receptive audience present. Given our isolated situation I felt it was unrealistic and out of place to celebrate any of the many splendid festivals.

As if by magic, a solution to this problem came my way by a chance flick of a switch. As I turned the television on one Sunday morning to watch *Nai Zindgi, Naya Jeevan*, an Asian magazine programme, there was a Colonel Gregory being interviewed by the programme presenter. Colonel Gregory was explaining about Comex-10, the tenth Commonwealth expedition to India, being mounted as a memorial to the late Lord Mountbatten. The main aim of these expeditions had been to get people of different nations together in order to break through the racial barriers that divide them.

On Monday evening Khush and I went to the Comex Club in London, to be interviewed by Colonel Gregory. At first he was very apprehensive. He had never taken anyone younger than seventeen before. We talked a lot about race relations and the unique role that the younger generation could play. He was finally convinced of my sincerity and agreed to take Khushwant provided someone from the team would agree to take charge of Khush, who was only thirteen at the time. I note my very grateful thanks here to Sardar Manjeet Singh Kajal, Colonel Gregory's secretary, who volunteered to take Khushwant under his wing. The expedition was to take the form of a train journey for seven weeks from Simla in the north to Ooty in the south, spanning some four thousand miles. Khushwant was overjoyed at the thought of playing his violin in the self-scripted entertainment that the expedition was to provide throughout its journey.

The final contingent consisted of delegations of about ten people each from Zambia, Canada, England and India. Here at last was one dream come true for my son, this trip of a lifetime, in the words of Anne Murray, secretary of Comex-10, 'an opportunity for young people of the Commonwealth to demonstrate that you do not get to know another man by bullying, frightening or humiliating him, but by understanding what ticks inside.' Both Darshan and I felt that the cost of the trip, some five hundred pounds, was a very low price to pay for such a high-grade educational experience.

In October 1980 my young son set out on his adventurous train ride across India while the three of us waited at home, praying for his well-being and eagerly awaiting the post every morning. Needless to say, it truly was a memorable journey for Khushwant. He could hardly believe the contrasts in the geography of the land, from the cool and fresh climate of Simla down to the hot and dusty plains of the south. The strong overtones of the ancient culture pervasive in both modern and traditional schools and colleges intrigued him. They travelled from Simla to Ludhiana to Chandigarh and down to Ooty. Every single day was an exciting new experience. Khushwant was discovering India, my homeland, in the best possible way. Everywhere a warm reception awaited them, whether they went to have tea with the Governor of Himachal Pradesh or to a concert in an ordinary state school; whether they watched sport as honoured guests at Ludhiana or simply wandered around as tourists in Chandigarh, India's most modern city. Khush experienced the soul-awakening experience of sleeping under the giant canopy of the stars. Like a magic wand the warm hospitality of the Indian people transformed his distorted image of India for ever. The contrast between the wealthy and the poor there has to be seen to be believed; the experience redefined the word 'poverty' for him. He also acquired an understanding of the depth of the psychological connection that exists between the English and the Indians. He was quite taken aback by the beautiful churches, both in Simla and Ooty, by the cosmopolitan lifestyle everywhere. At first hand he experienced a truly multi-cultural and multi-racial society. Perhaps one day, my son may want to write about his experience of the breathtaking splendour of the Nilgiri mountains or the cyclones and landslides they narrowly missed in Madras.

The members of the expedition were presented to Prince Philip on their return at the Commonwealth Institute in London. Our journey to the Commonwealth Institute in December 1980 was riddled with ill-luck. Despite my disapproval, Darshan had insisted on going by car as he had driven to that part of London many times before. I wanted us to go by train as the catheter inserted in his abdomen might have made him extremely uncomfortable. We had started from home at half past eight to give us ample time for a steady journey. Ill-fated and star-crossed, we got caught in a traffic jam near Uxbridge.

Darshan lost all control. To avoid the increasingly congested traffic, he turned into a country lane. Winding and narrow, it presented us with one hazard after another. Suddenly, we had gone crash and bang into the back of a Volkswagen. Darshan got out of the car and swore blindly at the woman driver. It was our fault, and it would have been far more sensible to admit it. The owner of the Volkswagen was equally adamant and stood there taking all the details. There was not a telephone box in sight. I pleaded with her to let us go, and explained the situation to her. When she did finally move her car out of the way, Darshan headed straight for the motorway. Only it was in the opposite direction. We both realised this simultaneously. He yelled out a most appalling set of words in Punjabi and then I heard him shout, 'Hold on! I am going to do a U-turn!'

'Open the door and roll on to the hard shoulder, Khush!' I screamed, gripped with fear. A U-turn on a motorway? Had I heard him right? As both the doors opened, Darshan pulled Khushwant towards him and did an emergency stop, throwing us both forward in our seats. As soon as the car had stopped, our instantaneous reaction was to get out. Khush clutched me, crying bitterly with anger and humiliation, while Darshan swore at us.

Under different circumstances, I would never have got back into the car, but I was dressed in a flimsy silk sari, and the cold wind of mid-December was cutting right through my bones. Besides, if I kept my peace, there was still a faint chance of getting to the presentation on time. Perhaps that day had dawned under an evil star. The car barely managed to roll to the next exit. The radiator had burst. I heard a shrill hiss and the car came to a halt. The engine had gone dead. In a sombre, panic-stricken state of mind, I simply walked away, holding Khushwant's hand, not knowing where we were, or what to do. We must have gone a few hundred yards when Khush noticed a taxi in the distance. The taxi driver was very kind and accepted a promissory note of payment. Time was pressing. I was extremely angry. For a moment I thought of going straight on. But I could not leave my husband stranded: his dialysis change was due soon. We went back to pick him up. I said nothing but prayed fervently.

We made it just ten minutes before the ceremony began. Ten Green Pennants were awarded to those people who had most helped the Comex Expedition. This award, designed for adventurous activities, bears Prince Philip's personal cipher on one side and the wheel of law, from the Ashoka Pillar of Sarnath, India, on the other. The prodigious feelings of pride as Khushwant shook hands with Prince Philip brought floods of tears to my eyes. My son had nearly been robbed of his very special moment. If that had happened, I would never have forgiven myself. Perhaps the time had come to take a firmer stand on decisions which I believed to be right, which were dictated by common sense. My husband's aggressive and parochial stand in taking all the decisions had nearly cost us our lives. What would have been the consequence of such meaningless self-destruction for our five-year-old, who was waiting behind with a child-minder? The time had come to assert myself positively.

That day, I took my first step. While Darshan decided to stay the night with his brother in Slough, Khush and I returned home to Milton Keynes on the train. As the boys and I sat down to dinner, and we reflected upon the previous day's events, I knew that another stage in the metamorphosis of my personality had been completed.

For peritoneal dialysis to be a successful form of treatment, tremendous patience on the part of the patient is required. Despite meticulous preparation before the inlet tube is attached to the P.D. bag, there is a tendency for air bubbles to form, thus causing obstruction to the flow. Every time this happened, Darshan's temper got out of control. We would hear him stamping on the floor and swearing, but we were not allowed near him. One winter day in early January, when this happened, he was in such distress that I offered to drive him to the hospital. I had not passed my test, but could have driven him slowly and safely. He refused and drove himself, in a pair of pyjamas, all the way to Oxford. The car broke down about two hundred yards from the Churchill Hospital.

There were many such incidents which widened the rift between Darshan and myself. Though the boys understood and sympathised with his condition, neither of them could come to terms with his outbursts of anger at us. I kept encouraging the children to look beyond his illness, and see that it was not Daddy's fault. But a child's response in love soon turns to rejection if he is subjected to constant hostility. There is also a major cultural difference here. An English child is 'asked' whereas an Indian child is 'told' concerning various errands. Darshan saw no earthly reason for ever 'asking' his sons or even saying 'please'. Added to this was his insistence upon referring to Khush as 'bastard' with every demand. Whenever I felt that the situation between father and sons was reaching explosion point, I would step in and fulfil his demands myself. It was simply to restore some semblance of calm, but my husband's view was that I was spoiling the boys. Khush and Arune said that I had no right to ask them to become Daddy's servants just because I had let myself be a slave to him all my married life.

The other main problem with the dialysis treatment was that of weight gain. There was no chance of Darshan being considered for a kidney and pancreas transplant unless his weight was steady. I felt desperately sorry for my husband, who had always been so fond of food. As more dietary restrictions were imposed, Darshan's sense of thirst and hunger became heightened. Every night, he would wake me up and demand jam and banana sandwiches. He would insist that he was going into a coma and that, if I did not oblige, he would just lie there and die. I had been told that there was very little chance of a coma while a patient was on P.D., but that if he did experience the symptoms, he should swallow a few dextrose tables. Every night we quarrelled over this. Gradually, contact and conversation between us became minimal. I carried on obliging his midnight demands. He had become too engrossed in his illness to notice that I found it all very exhausting.

I had also started to resent the ever-increasing dependence of the boys on me. Every day, I attempted to set up situations which would push the boys in the direction of their father. It was easier to do this with Arune, who was still at an impressionable age, but it was not to yield any response from Khushwant. Arune, too, openly declared war on us, as he felt hurt and confused by both Darshan and me. He started to display a clear preference for Khushwant's company to either of ours. He followed his big brother everywhere. I guess that the self-preservation instinct of a child was quick to find a solution.

Though Arune would hardly speak to me during the day, at night it was a different story. Most of his asthma attacks came at night. Then he would only be comforted by lying on my tummy. I would lie awake, trying to figure a way out, gently lulling Arune back to sleep. I decided not to pressurise my sons any more. These young lives entrusted to me by destiny deserved to be nurtured with care, not pushed about and bullied in a tug of war between two selfish parents. So long as they had the full support and enthusiasm of one parent behind them, their well-being would be ensured. 'I must never fail them,' I said aloud to myself time and again.

Perhaps we should have sought help from an outside agency at that stage, but for both of us interference from a stranger would have been problematic. Back home, I had never come across such ideas. From early childhood, one learnt to relate to uncles, aunts and grandparents just as closely and naturally as one did to parents, and brothers and sisters. Differences, discord, disagreement and dissension were never openly expressed outside the family. That would have made people talk, which would blemish a family's *izzat*. These are some of the reasons why, to an outsider, an Indian family would always seem to be organised, whole and functioning perfectly as a unit.

I was quite prepared though to seek counsel from the medical social worker at the Churchill Hospital. She had often talked with Darshan and me about the social side of things for a renal patient. Alas! My suggestion made Darshan so angry that he stopped seeing the social worker altogether.

Physical contact between Darshan and me was virtually non-existent. It gave my husband ample opportunity to taunt me. Yet again the fault lay with me. He blamed his lack of desire on to me and not his complicated prognosis. I felt very guilty at having deprived him of a wife's loving response in those most intimate of moments. Darshan seemed permanently angry with himself and the world. He started having long conversations on the phone with his friends and relatives about the complexity of his condition. He was always full of self-pity.

A lot of my English friends had adopted yoga and meditation as a means of relaxation. Because of my Sikh upbringing, yoga, a Hindu form of discipline, did not have any appeal. I resorted to prayer and exercise to keep my muscles and mind in control. There seemed no alternative in sight. My existence seemed to be solely for my husband's convenience.

In January 1981, Darshan's nephew asked to come and stay in our house for a few months with his wife and baby. Tarsem had found a job in Milton Keynes and was hoping to be allocated a corporation home in due course of time. If we could let them live with us until then, they would be able to save enough money to start life on a secure basis in Milton Keynes. They were Darshan's close relatives and, of course, we had to accommodate them. Darshan offered them the main bedroom and told me to share the bunk beds with Khush and Arune. How much would their stay interfere with our lives? What about the increased risk of infection as more people shared the same washing facilities? Nothing was discussed. The whole episode left me completely baffled. Why was my husband insistent upon destroying our lives? 'Prognosis of a renal failure is never very encouraging. Coupled with diabetes, it leaves very little room for manoeuvre.' The renal specialist had spelt it out for us. Why then was Darshan not taking any steps whatsoever to stabilise his condition? How much more responsibility could I take? Every night, the young people played with their baby till eleven o'clock while Arune, Khush and I tried to sleep. Our mealtimes simply did not suit them. The boys had no choice over their favourite television programmes any more as the video was on all day, showing one Indian movie after another. When I did ask Darshan to sit and discuss all these living arrangements, I got a mouthful of verbal abuse along with a bruise on my forehead.

For me that was the end of all guilt and responsibility towards my husband. This was not a marriage any more, and perhaps the time had come to put an end to it. I could no longer disentangle the web of misunderstanding and disharmony. It seemed to me that, even if my husband was at death's door, his relatives would have the first claim to his attentions. Something inside my confused mind had snapped and, try as hard as I could, I was running out of sympathy for Darshan.

It was through Darshan's nephew Tarsem that I met Meena and Narinder. Dr Menaka Patel (referred to affectionately as Meena) did not have any close relatives in this country. She was a registrar psychiatrist in London. Hitherto I had not been able to exchange my innermost thoughts with anyone. With Meena I developed that very rare bond of friendship. We came to relate to each other in many ways, and she shared and eased the tension of many of my distressing moments.

It was becoming increasingly difficult to bring Darshan out of the hypoglycaemic comas which he went into frequently. The superficial veins used for injection of dextrose were getting thrombosed (clotted) at an alarming rate. Doctors from the local practice who were called out by me between three and four times a week were insistent that either the dose of insulin being administered to Darshan had not been calculated correctly by the hospital, or there was something drastically wrong with his diet. I did not have the courage to say to them that my husband's intake of insulin and food were being decided entirely by himself with total disregard to the specialists.

My determination to stop my marriage from becoming a statistic was now wavering. Darshan's condition was deteriorating rapidly. Every blood and urine test showed a dangerous imbalance of the trace elements. Each consecutive coma was longer than before, depriving his brain of precious oxygen, damaging it a little, probably irreversibly, each time. On one such occasion, when a doctor from the local practice sat searching for a vein from ten in the evening to two in the morning, I decided to give Darshan an ultimatum. 'I would like to have an appointment to see the specialist. I want an explanation of your condition and unless you agree to let me see to your medicine and diet precisely according to the instructions of the specialists, I am going to leave you.' At best, he might realise that invalidity and mental incapacity would result if he carried on. At worst he would hit me, showering me with his glorious Punjabi diction. He took the second route.

'Take your bloody children and go wherever you like!' Digging his elbows into my ribs, he pushed me out of the way.

'They are your children too. If you want us to leave, then let us do it honourably. I have nowhere to go. I can't stay here any longer and watch you kill yourself slowly.'

Whatever his reasons for doing such damage to himself, I had no physical strength left to pick up the pieces. Of all the dark clouds looming over the horizon, finance was the most frightening one. I had never been allowed a separate bank account. There were two small savings accounts for the children. Insurances, mortgage, endowment policies, were all in our joint names and Darshan held all the documents under lock and key.

It all seemed—well, insane. I took another of my long walks and thought everything out carefully. I wanted so much to discuss my decision with my mother. But the one who had always supported me with long, comforting letters of hope, did not write any more. Every morning, for months, I ran downstairs, often tripping, to get the mail as soon as I had heard the postman's knock. I lay awake many nights, trying to figure out her change of heart. After all, she had witnessed my agony for a whole four months.

I thought that once we had moved to a bigger house, and nearer Darshan's work, the pressures of transport and space would ease and Darshan's attitude would relax. In March 1981, on our fifteenth wedding anniversary, we moved to Parkside, Furzton. Alas! Nothing changed at all. His relatives continued to live off my goodwill and our resources, while the last few remaining shreds of hope slowly but surely crumbled around me. I did not feel the need to uphold the glorious façade of *izzat* any longer for the benefit of relatives and friends. There had to be more to life.

14

My Miracle

My relationship with Darshan was now in name only. I lived a separate existence under the same roof. At times I wondered what it was like to love or be loved. That rapturous, exalted feeling lay buried inside me somewhere. My soul, my mind, trapped inside a body, had gone on hour after hour, day by day for years, searching for the love I had lost. I had not given up the cherished dream of finding Aziz, the dream of setting myself free. I would remind myself of the circumstances under which I was parted from the one I had loved. The elders of the family, in the name of *izzat*, had walked me round a holy book four times and had said, 'From this day on, this stranger, Sardar Darshan Singh Jabble, is your husband. You shall obey and worship him.' Nowhere in a Sikh or Hindu wedding ceremony do the scriptures lay down the rules by which a husband should abide. They had invoked Guru Nanak and Guru Gobind Singh to the defence of their act. I was told in front of the whole congregation that the purity and sanctity of my soul had been preserved just in time.

Like a ghost, the memory of the nineteenth and twentieth years of my life had gone on haunting me. Not for a day had I felt that Darshan was my soul-mate, my partner, my husband. He had called me names like 'fridge' and 'icebox' so many times that I had actively sought out means to rectify my unresponsive sexuality. Was it true? One could train oneself to observe all kinds of disciplines, but could feelings of love ever be dictated? For me, love and sex were two parts of the same oneness. Aziz and his love had been an integral part of me for two years. Every moment was deeply etched on my memory. How could a part of oneself be put away and forgotten just because of time and physical barriers?

In my thousands of hours of loneliness, I had tried to reach out to

Aziz for comfort, for love, and then cried myself to sleep, glad that every night had brought me nearer death. Perhaps naïvety came into play here. First Khush and then Arune had filled that void. For a while they had kept me from going insane. Motherhood was a constant challenge, always full of surprises. In rising to the occasion it was easy to forget my own inner struggle. But the boys were growing up and my restlessness was making me thoroughly miserable. Meena would often suggest that I should relax my puritanical attitude a little, and maybe seek psychiatric advice.

It was during one of these melancholy, sullen moods, in February 1981, that I had gone to the central Milton Keynes library. Back in 1972, when I had gone to India, an old classmate had told me that Aziz had completed his medical studies and had gone to England, though he did not know exactly where. Ever since mother had left, I had come to the library often, looking through the telephone directories of various cities just in case I'd strike lucky, somehow, somewhere. The librarian must have noticed the despair on my face during my frequent visits. She asked me if she could help. It was so funny. I had tried so hard that I had missed the one very obvious place—the Medical Directory. Despite the 'Silence Please' sign, we risked a chuckle. There it was! His name, his address in Manchester. I thanked the librarian and, trying hard to keep my racing heart still, I walked up and down the boulevards all afternoon. I did not know what the next step would be. This was one occasion when I had to harness my impulsive, impetuous heart and simply think, again and again.

During July 1981 I revealed my internal turmoil to Meena. Were they simply juvenile feelings of romantic love haunting me? Was destiny leading me towards self-destruction? Was there any logic or rationale in my decision to go and see Aziz! She did not ridicule me, but reassured me that if I did not go I would never be able to decide on the direction of my future life. So long as I was aware of all possible outcomes and their consequences, I would be able to handle the meeting.

What about Aziz though? Wouldn't it be selfish of me to disturb what might be a happy, contented marriage? I knew that his wife too, was a doctor. Next to his name in the Medical Directory, was listed a woman of the same name and address. But if their marriage was happy and stable, then surely seeing me again would not make much difference? In Meena's professional opinion, my feelings for Aziz, my past and the resulting inhibitions would go on producing sacrificial tendencies and I'd never be free to make any new relationship, unless I did go and see him. She said that I would have to be prepared for his rejection and refusal to see me if he saw my intrusion in his life as a threat.

So, without any preconception of what was about to happen, I arrived in Manchester on 18 October 1981. I had booked a place at a women's hostel. I had written a small note to Aziz but had not had the courage to post it until the previous day.

It was difficult to sleep that night. I was afraid of what might be unleashed in both of us. Somewhere in that city was his house. Somewhere else was his surgery. He would be getting up in a while to go to the surgery: I knew that much. It was his duty that morning. I felt very foolish and presumptuous. 'Use your common-sense. Are you mad? Have you ever heard such nonsense before? You'll never be able to retrace these steps. For the love of God, go back to Milton Keynes.' Logically, it all sounded so unwise. But I could not go back. Not after torturing myself for nearly ten months to come that far.

The walk from the women's hostel to his surgery was the longest I have ever taken. 'Are you the lady who rang from Milton Keynes last week?' The receptionist made Milton Keynes sound so foreign.

'Yes, I am. Please will you tell Dr Aziz that an old friend is here to see him,' I almost whispered rather coyly.

'I am sorry, lass, but he is at the other surgery today. There was a last minute change in his plans.'

I was relieved in a way, for it gave me time to collect my thoughts and calm down a little.

I called for a taxi. At the surgery, I requested the receptionist to simply let me go in as the next patient. I wanted to surprise him. He rang for the next patient. I knocked on the door. I entered quietly at his response to my knock and gently closed the door behind me. Without lifting his head from the prescription that he was writing at the time, he pointed to the chair. The moment of truth had arrived. I stood frozen. Then he lifted up his face. There was instant recognition. His pen fell from his hands.

'*Shanno Tum*'—and then a pause—'*Kahan se aaye?*' 'Where did you come from?', 'My goodness! You have become so thin.' Like me, he too must have had difficulty in moving. '*Aayo! betho.*' 'Come and sit here.'

So I walked towards him. He stretched out his arms and we held each other tight, simply shaking.

'Did you think I could forget—ever?' Out of all the most exciting words in the English dictionary, that was all I could summon to my command in those moments of utterly euphoric exultation.

'I searched for you everywhere, really I did . . . ' Then he bombarded me with questions. Where was I staying? Did I live in Manchester? How had I come? Had I had any breakfast? Was it really me?

I didn't get a chance to answer as the receptionist rang through to remind him about the waiting patients. So we had to let go, compose ourselves, and I waited in the receptionist's room while he finished his appointments.

I closed my eyes and pretended that it was a dream. Sixteen years had elapsed since we had been parted. He was talking to me as if only yesterday he had kissed me goodbye at the Buddha Jayanti Park, New Delhi, promising to see me again. It was crazy! 'Any time now, someone's going to wake me!,' I thought.

After he had finished, we went for coffee and then for a walk by a river. Every atom in my whole being was most incredibly elated. I wanted to scream and shout, 'Hey, Manchester! You are simply the most wonderful, the most gorgeous city in the whole wide world!'

Aziz looked at me. There was nothing missing. With all my tenderness I had loved him. 'Hey! what do you think of this then? I found you, didn't I?' And then he told me how he had tried to approach everyone that he knew, officials in high places, to show them the marriage certificate and stop my wedding. But no one had wanted to help him. A marriage between a Sikh and a Muslim! Everyone had thought it so ridiculous. And his audacity to ask for help! What did he think they could do, kidnap me and help cause a communal riot? In a land where tradition and religion dictate life-styles to such extremes what did he hope to achieve? The memory of the Sikh-Muslim Riots during the Partition and after lingered on.

That day was ours and I wanted to relish every minute. I had defied the cruel traditions; I had defied time and distance. The sun's rays were dancing and shimmering on the river. I felt so alive. We had touched each other's lives again. I could hardly believe that it was happening. For years, I had kept this loss concealed, had tried to forget it. Every so often, a little happening, an odour or chance remark would break through my defences and the concealed pain would come to the surface. I had kept my dream so very private. It had been so long and so lonely. But why was I suddenly feeling so gloomy? Wasn't it a time for rejoicing? Perhaps it was that feeling of anti-climax.

'If only your father could see us now!'

'No, Aziz! No bitterness, please. It's an ugly feeling. Today, I forgive them all. Today, I know somewhere up there is Rab, keeping an eye on me.'

'I want to make it up to you. I wish I could marry you, but my children are so young. I too had an arranged marriage. She does not match my nature at all.'

I put my fingers on his lips then. I had not found him out to destroy his marriage. Muslim men are allowed up to four wives. That part of it would have been easy if I had allowed it. I was glad that he had married. I had only wanted to untangle my own spider's web of memories and related emotion. It had been like a crippling disease of the mind. I would never let him destroy his marriage or his relationship with his children on my account. I did not wish to be wife number two. I would accept my destiny, my loneliness, provided I could look forward to being with him two to three times a year.

'Why don't you study to be a doctor now? I'd pay for the tuition fees.' He made me laugh by his insistence that, once I was divorced, I should pick up my studies where I had left off.

Then we talked about our children. His children went to a private school. Naturally, better financial circumstances had made available all kinds of exclusive opportunities. Despite all odds, I had never let my boys down either.

'I don't know whether I have your kind of courage but I'll do my best to make it up to you. Don't ever run away from me again, Shanno! I haven't got over the last time yet.'

And the magic of our togetherness engulfed me once again.

Khush had been very confused by this sudden trip that I had taken. He was waiting for an explanation. Upon my return I told him the truth as best I could. Khush had heard about my past briefly. It was important to me that my adolescent son should understand my point of view.

His reply nearly choked me. He hugged me and said, 'Mummy! I am so happy that you have found Aziz and you two love each other. You'll marry of course, after the divorce, won't you?' My young son had grown up and become a friend. How lucky I felt then, how grateful.

He said that it was a bit old-fashioned and unrealistic to go on living apart and yet love Aziz. In retrospect now, my feelings of commitment must have sounded ridiculous to Khush. Khushwant's ideology on love and marriage is a sort of half-way house between East and West. 'How can he care for you from so far away? If you love each other, surely you'd want to be together.'

I could disregard public opinion, especially gossip at the Gurudwara and ridicule from the Punjabi families in the city. I could ignore my parent's rejection of me, which would no doubt follow. But how would I learn to disregard the demands of my mortal soul and human body. Feelings I thought did not exist within me had been awakened in all their entirety. Most of the day would pass by quietly, with a song on my lips and an incredible joy in my heart. I'd hear Aziz's voice on the telephone and all depression would leave me. Whenever we met, I'd make it a most wonderful time for both of us, magical moments of pure joy, I promised myself. I had nurtured and nourished this dream with most desperate prayers. Destiny had given me a second chance. Only a fool would throw a second chance away.

Suddenly, I wanted to do so much. I wanted to study further to improve my qualifications so that I could work with women and girls in similar situations to myself. There were many; I knew that from the regular reports in various newspapers and books. I wanted to do some research. I was sure (and still am) that somehow I'd be able to find a vocation in this field. Life had been kinder to me than to many. Though my efforts at further education had been sporadic, they could now be unified, once the present drama and commotion were over. I was determined to give my future career a better structure. Mine was not a fairy story to end happily ever after but I would make sure that I made no more compromises regarding my future. My miracle would help me to come out of my purgatorial existence, so that I could be free to make my own decisions and my own mistakes. The whole of my past was dictated by tradition. I had lived a double life from dawn to dusk, satisfying someone else's needs. I would not let my future be designed by someone else. I would simply cherish the few precious moments I could spend with Aziz. It felt so good to be in his company.

I had introduced Aziz to Arune as my 'special friend'. How difficult we find it, as adults, to explain certain aspects of life to children, and yet many of them simply accept it, so long as they know that nothing is going to disturb their secure world of love and toys and play. Arune had cuddled up to me one morning and had said, 'Do you want to marry your "special friend" Mummy?' I said that I could think of nothing better or nicer, but that could never be as he was already married. Though my little son has never prodded me about the same thing again, I believe the incident introduced him to the contradictory world of adults. What we advocate as values to our children we often fail to inculcate into our own lives. I had always encouraged the boys towards 'independent thinking', teaching them at the same time to show respect for other people's opinions. This and many other attitudes of my unconventional life had impregnated their thinking. To Khushwant's western way of thinking, I had not resolved my dilemma at all. I had imprisoned myself in a new, never-ending torment. Then, I thought he was just being protective towards his mother, not wanting to see her hurt any more. Now, I know how right he was.

Pangs of doubt, of indescribable fear of losing Aziz arose again. In mid-December he came down to London for a day to be with me. His flight was late by a couple of hours. Waiting was sheer torture. For five heavenly, blissfully happy hours we were together again. All the feelings of contentment I had ever experienced were with this man alone.

'See! I have made you beautiful again!' His warm touch and gentle smile had made me tingle right through. It was a new beginning for me. He was the keeper of my deepest emotions. That was his only commitment and responsibility towards me.

Perhaps the loudest noise in the world is made by silence. To protect Aziz's privacy and my own, I had wanted to stay silent. Besides, concepts such as love, devotion, have new definitions, new meanings today. Who would have understood if I had tried to explain? It wasn't going to affect anyone else's life anyway. Mother and my brother wrote a succession of letters asking for explanations. I did not owe anyone any justification for my actions. I felt silence was the best course to adopt.

The day that I received the result of the pregnancy test as being positive I had at first trembled and felt embarrassed. Then overwhelming emotion had surged within me. Yes, of course! That was to be my answer. I had always wanted more children. A part of him growing inside me—what a beautiful manifestation of an incredible dream—a living form of our love. I felt good. That would be my salvation, to live out my agony in bringing up our baby. I would find strength to combat the grief of separation and loneliness. I was not afraid of financial hardship. I had had good practice at doing with the bare minimum. I tried to figure out the situation at school. It seemed workable. Mr Clarke said that I was entitled to maternity leave like everyone else and that my job would be kept open. I wanted to sort everything out independently. I would never let myself and the baby become a liability for Aziz. I would make it the most beautiful event of my life.

When I told Aziz, at first he was frightened for me. Then he laughed at my optimism and thought me very brave but utterly mad. Later in the week, there was a firm and loving assurance in his letter that I was to keep him informed. It was good to know that he was there to turn to, if I needed to.

Towards the end of December, while going to the solicitor, I slipped on ice and fell downhill on a steep slope. All my hopes about the baby were about to come to an end. I woke up the following morning with excruciating pain in my back, and feeling a little feverish. My doctor warned me about a possible miscarriage. It couldn't be. 'What should I do? Please tell me—anything—just tell me and I'll do it.' I was going mad with fear and confusion. Dr Anand tried to calm and comfort me by putting forward a lot of logical and very sensible explanations. It might have been just the fall. There might have been something wrong with the foetus. It was nature's way of getting rid of a malformed foetus. It was a good thing, he said. A good thing? I thought my mind would explode! Why? I considered myself a healthy woman. Khush and Arune were two perfectly normal healthy pregnancies.

Dr Anand got quite angry with me. 'Aren't you asking too much of yourself? Do you not think that the stress and the strain of your present circumstances is going to have any effect on you? I know you like to think so, but you are not made of steel. You are human, like the rest of us, you know.'

Why was he scolding me? He should have been sympathetic. Everything was wrong. I lay in bed and rested for the next six days. The bleeding was persistent and kept getting heavier. On the morning of the 29 December, I lost the baby. I washed the foetus and put it in a dish to take to the doctor, as he had asked. By midday, he had arranged for me to go to Northampton General Hospital to have the womb scraped and cleaned. Until then, I had never thought anything would defeat me, that anything could send me down into the deep, dark dungeon of depression. Was it all an illusion I was chasing? Uncertainty had raised its ugly head once again.

Darshan had realised that something quite new had happened, quite separate from the existing marital chaos. He had heard me pleading with Dr Anand to advise me how to save the baby. As a result, the tension in my marital situation had accentuated and accelerated beyond all bounds. He made all kinds of threats. Though, in my view, my marriage had never really existed and had certainly ended a long time ago, I suppose it was justified from his point of view to want to crucify and persecute me. There was a forest of troubles looming over the horizon. I yearned to experience the strength and comfort of Aziz's arms around me but it seemed that I had to find a solution alone.

The following Sunday at the Gurudwara, Darshan spread it around that I had been pregnant with an illegitimate child and I had gone to the hospital to get an abortion done. In her next letter Mother, who had obviously been ill-informed by Darshan, wrote some disgusting accusations and compared me to a dirty dung beetle. Darshan's vindictive spreading of misconstrued facts made it impossible to talk to anyone any more. Some Asian women friends who were at first sympathetic no longer wanted anything to do with me. Everyone had shut me out. I had violated the sanctity of marriage. I had played foul and cheated my poor sick, disabled husband.

And where was Aziz? Sharp knives of conflict and confusion were starting to cut through me. I was looking in the wrong direction for comfort. Every atom in my being hurt. Aziz had also said that it would have been impractical, difficult, if the baby had survived. 'Think with your brain, not your heart,' he said. On the path of life, my feet had been ridden with so many splinters I had felt them bleeding. I had limped, but never given up hope of finding him. Where was he now? Why could he have not uttered a few kind words instead of telling me to face reality? I had never had any security in my marriage, yet I had walked on, hoping always. Is that how it was always going to be? Why did the happiness of a few moments always have to be paid for with separation and the grief of a thousand? I felt I was burning brightly in pain, so that all that poisonous bitterness and tension and passion would burn out from within me. Nothing had really been resolved. A child could have been the embodiment of all that was unsaid, left unexpressed for years, a justification for my existence. Yet now there was nothing but pain and despair. Where would I get the strength to face callous and despicable remarks from all those nosey and spiteful relatives? I did not know.

Khushwant had known about my disappointment. He should have guessed that it was too deep a hurt for his mother, too private, and she wanted to be left alone.

'Let's go for a bike ride, Mummy, please.'

Reluctantly, I agreed to go with them. Away from the house, on the path by a play area, they both stopped. I sat on a bench while they played around.

'Don't be sad, Mummy. You have us.'

Suddenly, they had both thrown their arms around me. The only two people whose judgement really mattered had declared it in a few simple words.

'And you two have me always, don't ever forget that. I will never, never let you down.' I kissed them both and tried a smile through the curtain of tears. What the hell was I looking and feeling so pathetic for? I had so many good things, so many blessings. I knew then that with two such strong supports I would build a future for us. We would come through, somehow, some day.

15

Heading Towards the Divorce

Divorce in Indian society is a dirty word, and a very rare event. For a woman to divorce a man is unheard of. For a woman to divorce a sick, disabled man would be adding insult to injury. I knew that if I proceeded with divorce on the grounds of unreasonable behaviour, for which more than enough evidence existed, I would be condemned to a life of isolation and complete rejection by the Sikh community of Milton Keynes. And what about the recrimination from my relatives in India, including my parents? They would close their eyes to the fact that I would be bringing up my children single-handed. I had already decided not to ask for any maintenance when the time came. For the majority of the women in the family it would be difficult to understand as they depended solely on their husbands economically. Their standards and status were determined by their husbands'. Much worse and more fearsome were the niggling doubts about my own ability to cope with the future as a single parent. But then, to all intents and purposes hadn't I been a single parent always?

I felt very sorry for Darshan who desperately needed someone to look after him. If he had answered one of the adverts in the matrimonial columns of the *Times of India* and had married a mindless moron who could have worshipped him unquestioningly, he wouldn't be in this predicament now. Instead he was almost on the verge of losing his dictatorship over me, losing it all. I am sure he had realised that I simply had had enough, for he had said that if I accepted the adultery charges, he'd divorce me. I'd have to tell him who Aziz was, and where he lived, as if this had been the only reason for divorce.

By his constant physical and verbal abuse, he had shown clearly that the children's feelings and reactions about his illness were inconsequential. Khushwant's offers of help were met by indignant innuendos. He had simply stopped listening.

One of the continuous arguments used to be over keeping a pet. Darshan hated cats, dogs, rabbits, the lot. One of my pupils, Stephen Searle, gave me the idea of building an aviary. He bred budgerigars as a hobby. A greengrocer neighbour had two spare pallets he let me have. Together Khush and I drew plans, bought some corrugated perspex, plywood and chicken mesh, and borrowed a relevant book from the library. As the technicalities of the construction were quite complicated, we were grateful to receive our neighbour's help. When the aviary was ready, we bought a pair of masked love-birds from the shop. Arune-Preet was very excited. He fetched his daddy by the hand and started to babble on about the birds.

'Your mother has failed miserably at everything else. She has no time to be a proper wife. So now she has decided to be a zoo keeper!'

I retorted that it was no skin off his back, and why did he always have to let the children see his misery?

I regretted my cutting remarks afterwards. But it was no good, we disliked each other intensely now. Even for the sake of the children, I could not go on making efforts at peaceful co-existence. Besides, such efforts have to be two-way. Our hatred for each other was spilling into our conversations with the children. My intuition and logic told me that the children would be better off out of this situation. Once again I remembered the *shabad* from the Adi Granth:

Take destiny in your own hands.
Have the courage of your convictions.
Life is precious and we only live once.

During February 1982, I made arrangements to go up to Manchester to see Aziz. I wanted to test out the reality of our feelings, which might only have been the result of a euphoric reunion. Khush was nearly fifteen and understood that his mother simply had to resolve the dilemma of the past by actually living through some of it or else she might end up as a psychiatric case. Valium would be the answer, but no permanent cure. I was aware of the signs of approaching depression and was determined to fight it. Khush knew that my past was like a dark night in which I lived, and dawn would never come until I faced my fears. 'Let things be. Accept the present as it is. What good is it waking up the dead?' All this advice was sound and rational, yet I could never rest until I had found out for myself.

The first two days were heavenly. We drove for hours. It was lovely to listen to his experiences in India. He seemed very successful, earning four times as much as I did. He had a huge five-bedroomed house and two cars, sent both his children to private schools, and bred parrots as a hobby. He and his wife went back to India for holidays every other year. The miracle of just sitting by him and his voice pouring into my ears felt overwhelming and thrilling. I was glad that life had been kind to him, that he had fulfilled his career ambitions.

'What about us, Aziz?'

'I love you and would make it up to you, you'll see. Meeting you is a miraculous dream come true.'

And he had held me tight. I felt secure, comforted and very reassured. I did not, dare not, ask *how* he could have made it up to me. I loved him so, because he was an honest, dependable and loving man. Such a man would not have hurt his young children or his wife for anything. And would I have wanted him to do so anyway? I think not.

The following two days were simply awful. His wife had got an inkling of my stay. He was unable to face her and was extremely tense and nervous. Suddenly it all felt dirty and ugly, not a miracle any more. I had trespassed on someone else's territory.

'Up to now I have been solely her property you see!' He sounded very agitated.

'You are a *person*. How can you describe yourself in these terms?' I protested.

'I am sorry! I won't be able to spend much time with you. Believe me, I want to. Sometimes I want to leave everything and run away, though I shall never be able to. My children are very young . . .'

Then there were tears. Questions and suspicions arose. What had I done? It was a very sad, very disturbing parting. He expressed regret time and again over his helplessness, envied me my courage and single-mindedness. We sat in his car quietly, just holding on to each other. His favourite tape played:

Hamari taraf se salam unko dena
Or keh dena unse salam aakhiri hai

Say goodbye to my beloved for me and
Tell her that it is my final greeting to her.

I came back from Manchester to a mountain of miseries. Khush had accepted Aziz's presence in my life, though he had stated his opinion quite clearly that it was sheer madness to wait for someone some hundred and fifty miles away. But a very unhappy Arune declared 'I hate this world Mummy, when you are not there.' A child's simple easy expression of his innermost feelings made me feel quite guilty.

I felt myself plunging deeper and deeper into a kind of insanity. I used to spend hours helplessly crying and wondering about the uncertainty of the future a second time around, the past tightening its grip around me and threatening to destroy not only me, but my children as well. I had to make a decision.

I decided to accept the adultery charges and urged Darshan to let the divorce go through. It didn't really matter how one put a final end to a marriage that had ceased to exist years ago. The whole Sikh community had passed their judgement on me anyway. In their eyes, I was a whore, a bitch, and a hundred different Punjabi words had been used to describe me. Basically they all meant a fallen woman. I should be excommunicated, some of them suggested. '*Isna apna moonh kala kiya?*' 'She has blackened her face. She should be burnt alive.'

Darshan said that he wouldn't have the satisfaction of punishing me in the Indian traditional way but he would make sure that little Arune was taken away from me, as an unfit mother. 'I don't want my son to grow up to be immoral.'

My knowledge of the law on all matters was still pretty raw. I borrowed a Reader's Digest book, *Know your Rights*, from a friend, and sat up all night reading the relevant details carefully. Under English law there was no question of anyone taking Arune away from me. There wasn't a single shred of evidence Darshan could have produced about my inefficiency or lack of caring as a mother. Motherhood had been my only joyful pastime in this wretched, condemned marriage.

The episode that took place in March 1982 put an end to all my dilemmas, doubts and guilt. It used to be my responsibility to pay the gas, telephone, electricity, water rates and children's expenses, together with any maintenance. Winter that year had been the worst for thirty-five years according to the newspaper reports. The gas bill for that quarter came to £176. This was followed by a huge telephone bill. Darshan had made a number of calls to India to consult barristers and lawyers in order to secure an order which would make it possible for him to have Arune's custody under Indian law.

After I finished my evening teaching, I went into the living room and asked Darshan if he would help pay those bills, as I couldn't possibly stretch my pay to accommodate either. He ignored me at first. When I pressed further for some sort of an answer, he got up suddenly and hit me violently with a clenched fist across the right ear three or four times. The whole room seemed to whirl around and it went completely silent. The pain was followed by a thundering, hammering noise which made me scream. Khush came bursting into the room. By that time I had fallen to the floor. Father and son exchanged strong words. I saw Khush go for the telephone in the hall. Darshan followed him. I got up and made a feeble attempt to intervene. Before I could reach either of them, the telephone had been ripped off the wall and Khush had gone next door to use their telephone. When he came back, trembling and angry, Darshan went for him.

'Where have you been, you bastard! Your bloody mother is all right. She doesn't need a doctor. She needs another of my fists.'

Khush screamed back, 'Don't you touch her!' and removed me from the scene. He sat me down, held my hands and waited.

The doctor came and confirmed that the right ear-drum had burst traumatically, but would heal reasonably well in five to six weeks, if proper care was taken. As he left, he said that he couldn't understand why I was putting up with such violence. On the way out he rebuked Darshan for his actions, who insisted that I had hurt myself because I attacked him and slipped in the struggle. I was not prepared to lie any more, so I gave the police an accurate and true statement.

Khush raised his voice to his father for the first time that night. 'If you ever raise your hand to Mother again, you can prepare yourself for the consequences.'

All in all, the whole drama petrified me. Beatings in the past had never injured me physically in so serious a way as to leave permanent damage. The following day I made my first visit to the solicitor. He secured legal aid and a protection order for me and the boys immediately. It was my first appearance in a Court of Law, a thoroughly unpleasant experience. I remember shaking and perspiring as if I were a criminal. I wanted to run away. The woman magistrate said I could take my time. It felt very wrong. What was I, a supposedly honourable, respectable member of society, doing in a Court of Law? Why did I have to go through that inquisition? The hearing finished by midday and to keep my mind quiet I went back to school. I knew, at least physically, that the boys and I were safe. Or were we?

The atmosphere got much worse at home from that day on. The boys and I locked ourselves in our rooms whenever Darshan was around, mainly to avoid confrontations. By mid-April, Darshan had given up work. He had accepted voluntary redundancy. He announced that he had no intention of proceeding with the divorce. It was my duty according to the Adi Granth and Indian law to look after him and obey him, no matter what the circumstances. He had sent for his father, his uncle and my father. They were all coming to teach me a lesson. To me these were all warning signs to somehow find a way out. My poor Arune! Being torn apart, locking ourselves in our own house like prisoners! Arune, whose cheerful chirping and humming used to fill my house, like the early morning birds, was now sad, quiet and tearful most of the time.

I had to carry on with my school job. Mr Clarke, head of the maths and science faculty, was most kind. He kept an eye on me but never interfered. His supportive concern saw me through many tense situations. School bells and children: together their noise was deafening, because it was amplified about two hundred times. He would see me grasp my ears in agony, and simply say 'Keep smiling! Keep your chin up. You are a brave girl.' I am sure his gentleness went a long way to helping me cope. My job was, in fact, my salvation. At that time it was much more than just a means to earn money. I carried on with my evening teaching; my students were the only people left with whom I had some contact. Even Meena was too frightened to come any more.

Darshan's behaviour was getting totally self-centred. Though he had stopped eating any of the meals I cooked, he would make as much mess as possible on and around the cooker, sink and fridge. I usually had to wait until after he had gone to sleep to clean up. The situation was desperate. I couldn't see any silver lining through the dark clouds on my horizon.

But I wasn't ready to give up.

16

My Exit

Since Darshan had given up work it was impossible for me to pay the mortgage and rates. He made a new will regarding his property in India. I argued that I had some right over it as I had contributed financially to our home over the last fifteen years. He said that the only way he would change his mind would be if I were to go back to India with the boys. He offered to buy our plane tickets.

'You are not fit to live here respectably. The Indian community considers you no more than a slut, a common tart,' he declared. How dare he? The anger and bitterness were building up to a pitch.

'You can keep your damned property! You cannot force me to go to India. This is my home and my children's! I shall make a life for myself and the boys here. I will show you! Just you wait and see!' I felt enraged. I would not let him tear my spirit to pieces. Let everyone make their disgusting accusations. 'What gives them the right to sit in judgement?' I thought, and felt very resentful.

In the days that followed, Darshan had his will altered legally, surrendered the life insurance policy, the children's endowment policies, and withdrew all the monies from the Post Office and building society accounts. He stopped the standing orders for the mortgage and rates and asked the estate agents to put the house up for sale.

I was very frightened. If the house were sold, where would the boys and I go? I begged him to discuss matters and come to some sensible arrangement. He refused to listen. I received a notice from his solicitor offering me five thousand pounds if I agreed to leave the house immediately. He was prepared to negotiate about the contents of the house but only through the solicitor. My solicitor's advice was that I should fight to keep the house only if I had the means to pay the mort gage. There was no law in the land that would throw a mother and two young children out from their own house; but, if I could not pay the mortgage, the building society would be compelled to repossess the property within six months. The only sensible course of action was to let the house be sold and to share the proceeds equally.

I made one last attempt at reconciliation with Darshan. The children did not deserve to become homeless. He said that the children were not his concern and anyway, they ought to realise what their mother was doing to them.

It's not often that I have contemplated suicide in my life. This was one occasion when I felt so inclined. I had always considered it a way out for cowards. Was I a coward? I could not just leave the boys to face life alone. I would have to end all three lives simultaneously. Otherwise what was I to do? Financially Darshan held all the cards. To whom could I have turned? Besides, I had never borrowed money before. No! Suicide was not for me. Perhaps I would have had the courage to end my own life, but I could never have touched the boys. I had good health, a steady job and two wonderful sons. As Grandma would have said, 'The problem that will defeat me, destiny has not designed yet.' After all, I could consider renting. We had lived in a rented flat before. I would find a solution, somehow. I remembered a similar fear that had gripped me, paralysed me once before, many years ago, when familiar and loved faces and places were exchanged for a cold, unfamiliar land. Had I not come through that triumphantly? I would do so again. I remembered Leo Tolstoy's words, 'The most difficult thing to do is to love life, even while one suffers, for to love life is to love God.'

One Sunday in April I woke up to an unusually loud, snoring noise coming from Darshan's bedroom. Whatever the consequences, both Khush and I decided to open his door and look. It was a horrific sight. He was lying prostrate, half on the floor and half on the bed, in a deep coma. Diabetics would know well that this state can easily be avoided by carefully controlled administration of insulin, and diet. The doctor came and gave him some injections and sent him to Northampton General Hospital. He had quite obviously tried to commit suicide.

Later I tried for the last time to talk to him via Arune. He slapped Arune, muttered some abuse and said, 'Tell your bloody mother that,

147

unless she agrees to go back to India, there will be no reconciliation'.

We couldn't visit him in the hospital again, as transport was becoming increasingly difficult to arrange. At my school, CSE examinations had started. The pressure was on. When Darshan came home from the hospital, I tried unsuccessfully to make some sort of compromise. His verbal abuse now included my parents back home, and his own brother and sister-in-law. In fact, anyone who tried to act as a mediator was told to keep out. Darshan hired the services of an Indian barrister who advised him that, if he could prove mental cruelty on my part, Arune-Preet could be taken away from me. The summary of the original five-page document is reproduced here, word for word:

'My wife has committed adultery. She is immoral and inadequate in her duties as a wife and mother. I have no job. My kidney problems have forced me to take voluntary retirement. My wife and children pester me constantly to take them shopping, to schools and leisure centres. Maybe they think I run a taxi service. She does not agree to sell the house. She is healthy and has a full-time job. She does not like to entertain or cook for my visitors. I cannot sleep at night with the lights off. They won't let me keep the lights on. She saves for the children regularly in a building society and declares that the money goes on grocery and bills. She says we should keep lodgers, when I can't bear to see my house being turned into a guest-house. My weight keeps changing due to my medical condition. I have to keep buying new clothes as she refuses to do the necessary alterations. She spends the evenings and weekends doing extra teaching or marking. She is incapable of cooking my special diet for me and makes me eat ordinary meals. We have not shared a bedroom for three years as she abhors physical contact with me. My wife writes abusive letters to my elderly parents, and does not like my relatives living in this country. She has money to spend on our older son's leisure activities such as violin lessons, but not to support my parents financially.'

He had stolen my passport and my British citizenship papers, my only identification. I decided to agree to sell the house. In June 1982 Darshan and I were legally separated. A detailed document was drafted. Until the sale of the house, all expenditure was to be shared equally.

Darshan was to pay the mortgage and general rates and I was responsible for water rates, gas, electricity, telephone, food and maintenance. I was to relinquish all claim to his property and money on my and the children's behalf. We were both instructed to do our utmost to ensure a speedy completion of the sale.

I did not press charges for an exclusion order. He had got what he wanted. Surely, he would want to cooperate now to speed matters up. The magistrate said that he would have to produce some real evidence if he wished to press charges of mental cruelty. There was nothing to substantiate my so-called lack of concern for the children and I was awarded their protective custody.

Some time during those days of despair and despondency, and the overwhelming set of arduous circumstances, I started to wake up to reality about my relationship with Aziz. In six months we had met only briefly, when he had come to London Airport to greet some relatives from India. Each time that I saw him I felt more of an intruder in his life. My grief at being separated from him had to remain private, mine alone for ever. It was wrong of me to ask for a share of his life. Our relationship was that of the soul and would stand by its own strength alone, he had said. Perhaps our relationship could exist on a platonic level?

At the end of July 1982, Darshan's father and uncle arrived from India. Naturally, I was apprehensive and wished I had somewhere else to go. Yet for the most part a warm and affectionate relationship developed between the three of us and Papaji. As long as I live, his reactions will astonish me. I had never talked to my father-in-law before. If I had stayed in India, our relationship could only have been one of distant and formal respect. He would have rarely seen my half-covered face because of *ghunghat*, the very strong tradition of covering one's face in the presence of in-laws, a form of *purdah* prevalent in most villages, even today. He would certainly have never conveyed anything to me directly. In the hierarchical structure of the joint family, he should have held the position of the highest authority. Instead, Bibijee's position was one of absolute dominance. Nothing could have restrained her hunger for power. Papaji was a very passive sort of man and remained aloof from it all, spending as much time at the mill as possible.

Our situation surprised him. He said that, from his son's letters, he was expecting to find a thoroughly lazy, modern and self-centred daughter-in-law. The boys and I took him on three trips—to London, Windsor and Blackpool. He was pleasantly surprised to find the boys obedient, respectful and polite. He had never seen the sea before. The illuminations at Blackpool fascinated him. He was embarrassed and disappointed by Darshan's behaviour. I told him that I was never ashamed of my love for Aziz, but that Aziz was married and had settled quite happily.

Since Mr Childs, my landlord at Chalfont St Peter had died, I had never talked so openly to anyone. For both the boys he was the world's greatest grandad. Just as they had managed to communicate with my mother, so they established a perfect rapport with Papaji. He was sorry that despite his state of health, Darshan was unapproachable when the subject of a reconciliation was brought up. Every night, they both talked till late. I guessed he was making an attempt to break through the abyss of silence which now existed between Darshan and me. Papaji did not once make an attempt to judge me.

1982 was the Festival of India year. Papaji accompanied us on all the different trips we made during August and September. I had made a fair attempt at integration, and though the boys did not speak Urdu or Punjabi, in lots of other ways their life-style was multi-cultural.

Most of the problems in our marriage had come about because of my husband's non-acceptance of changing circumstances and his illness. Papaji was, however, able to shed a little light on Darshan's total lack of interest even in projects which were usually 'a man's job'. Papaji had worked away from home at the mill and he said that the women at home had spoilt Darshan during his formative years, giving in to his every whim. He had never been expected to take his share of the tasks around the house.

Papaji was alarmed about Darshan's finances and was concerned that I was expected to look after him, bring up the children, and do a full-time job. It was understandable that I could not tolerate his vile abuse any more. Papaji said that I should do whatever was right for the children and myself. When all was said and done, I had total responsibility for the children. Neither set of grandparents could be of any practical help from so far away.

I shall always feel obliged to Mike Pickin, a physics master at Denbigh, for introducing me to the share ownership scheme operated by the Milton Keynes Development Corporation. Under the scheme, I would be able to buy a place of my own in joint partnership with the corporation. I did not need a deposit, only a steady job. The idea kept milling around in my head. It seemed like the perfect answer. I read all the available leaflets over and over to find some snags in the scheme. I could not find a single condition other than those which applied generally to all owner-occupied properties city-wide.

It all seemed too good to be true. Placing my faith in destiny, I went ahead and put my name down for the houses that were going to be released in August. Whatever one's strength of character, divorce and being a single parent bring their own peculiar set of problems. I did not want any additional ones because I was a woman and was not as conversant with property legislation as a man would have been in my position. So I carefully read the *Sex Discrimination Act* and the *Guide to Mortgages* issued by the Equal Opportunities Commission. I could not provide the standard of living that my sons had been accustomed to, but I could provide a measure of it—somewhere comfortable to live, somewhere calm and peaceful to return to at the end of the day.

The timing of the release of the houses in August was perfect. We were on holiday. During the whole of that week Arune was at the Woughton Campus Activities Scheme. If I wanted the house of my choice I would have to queue for the share ownership houses, which are issued on a first come, first served basis. On the Monday, after cycling Arune to the activities centre, I rushed to the housing office. A John Curry was already there, having arrived at seven o'clock. After getting some food I contacted Meena and another friend, Ron, to request help with sleeping arrangements. Cooking was no problem. John let us share his camping equipment. Meena and Ron agreed to park their cars for us to sleep in. Khush was a little upset the first night, and insisted that he would be the one to queue the following four nights. He was not at all happy with his mother sleeping outside with all kinds of strangers prowling around. Though I felt pretty secure with the car doors locked firmly, one learns not to argue with a teenage son who had grown up almost overnight and was anxious to take on the role of a mature and responsible adult. I decided that I would let Khush help me.

The following four days and four nights were tremendously exciting. The local paper did an article on us. We made all kinds of jokes about our queuing up. We must have looked so ridiculous, wrapped up in sleeping bags. Some actually said that we were mad; they wouldn't queue for a house even if they were paid to do it. The three of us, Khush, John, and I thought of it as a bit like waiting for Christmas. The weather was kind, the August sun shone every day, though the howling evening winds would easily have pushed me out of this competition if it had not been for Khushwant. Since then, many people have been known to queue up to secure a house under this marvellous scheme. Interest has grown and the last queuing was in mid-winter, with snow and temperatures below zero. On Saturday morning, absolutely exhausted, I signed and reserved a house. In the afternoon I said my 'thank you' to Khush, Ron and Meena at Milton Keynes Tandoori Restaurant.

Though Papaji was still with us, Darshan's general behaviour deteriorated rapidly. He was abusive verbally and physically in front of the children, using quite repugnant and indecent words. He wanted me to accept his offer of five thousand pounds and leave. He had started to set fire to various things in the kitchen. He was doing his own cooking now, leaving the kitchen in an utter mess, letting the pots of dal and curry boil over, throwing tea bags on the floor and sometimes being sick in the kitchen sink. Those days seemed like endless cleaning sessions. It had to be done, for Darshan's treatment of the property was fast making it unsaleable. He allowed his shampoo and toothpaste to spill on the bathroom carpet. He would frequently urinate on the carpet or empty the dialysis bags on the floor instead of in the lavatory bowl.

Papaji was getting desperate to go back home. At seventy-two, it was difficult for him to take much more. One afternoon I sat at the dinner table sorting out some work for school. Papaji and Darshan were in the living room enjoying a movie on television. Khushwant and Arune were out riding their bikes. Darshan came and sat beside me and started staring at me.

'Do you need any money?' he asked.

'No, thanks. Besides, our financial matters are separate now,' I replied quietly.

'I just thought if you need any money, I would take you upstairs, fuck you and give you twenty pounds. What do you say?'

I got up, trembling with fear and shame. He followed me into the kitchen and started bickering. I reminded him of the Protection Order and the non-molestation clause in it. At that point, Darshan flew into a rage and deliberately swept everything off the worktop. Grabbing hold of my hair he banged my head on the worktop several times, all the time muttering filthy abuse.

Poor Papaji! He had heard the scuffle. Shaking like a leaf, he tried to intervene. I struggled free and withdrew into my room for the rest of that day. Papaji's presence and participation in this most unpleasant scene caused me much sorrow and anguish. More than ever, I wished there was a relative we could go to just to remove ourselves from the situation.

Luckily, the following weekend Khush was going camping to Derbyshire with the school. Arune and I decided to go with them. For both Arune and me, climbing hills was a most exhilarating experience. It lifted our spirits and helped us to put the events of the last few weeks in proper perspective.

Most of us must sometimes act irrationally, particularly under strain. Perhaps this was the reason for my husband's actions. He wrote to his mother, 'Sharan-Jeet has taken on a rich lover. She has fought me in the courts and is now the legal owner of all my property. She will be coming to India shortly to instigate proceedings to throw you all out of the Giddarbaha House'. If he had written such a blatant lie to blacken my name, it did not make any sense, for in a few days we would be going our separate ways, once the divorce was through. I guessed that the whole situation was a crushing blow to his pride. Unable to hurt me, he had taken to inflicting hurt on the only person he had loved. It backfired in a most ridiculous way. The mother he had supported all his life sued him and sent him, by express delivery, a summons to appear before the court.

Even for his mother, Darshan could not swallow his pride and admit the truth. I heard him say to Papaji that he had issued a 'specific set of instructions to his solicitor' to fight the case. Though Papaji had realised the irrelevance of it all, I went to the solicitor and drafted a document, renouncing for myself and the boys rights to all properties and assets owned by Darshan. The document was witnessed and signed by Papaji and my solicitor. We sent it to Bibijee to assure her that, in truth, there was no case to fight. Though I do not consider myself a paragon of virtue, I can say in all honesty that I have never consciously contrived any wilful hurt on anyone. For the sake of the boys, it was of the utmost importance to conduct ourselves in an amicable, friendly manner. Darshan was driving us further and further away.

And then came the delightful news. The Youngs, the prospective buyers of our house, had managed to secure a mortgage. They wanted the contracts exchanged as soon as possible. They had asked for vacant possession of the property by 25 October. Darshan had been allocated a brand new flat at Oldbrook near the city centre and could move in when he was ready. As I was buying my house through the development corporation, I was given temporary accommodation at Netherfield. All seemed set to go ahead without any hitches. But it was not to be.

During the first week of October, Khush was away in Brittany with the Stantonbury Music Centre on an orchestral holiday. As soon as he returned, we were to move. The following Friday, when I returned home, I found the grill pan on fire. There was food, burnt to cinders, scattered around the cooker. In the living room, the fire was on full-blast and the wooden casing had been set alight by melted candle wax. The wax had travelled through into the elements filling the whole room with noxious fumes. Darshan had left me a note saying that under no circumstances would he sign the contract, unless I agreed to go to India. 'I would be kind to you. I would buy you a house. You can find a teaching job at Giddarbaha,' the note read. He had gone away somewhere, leaving no address. Of course the Youngs withdrew their offer.

He came back, a week later, with Papaji. Papaji was leaving for India in a couple of days and had come to say goodbye. Earlier Darshan had given Khush a camera in front of Papaji as a present. He asked Khush to give him back the camera as he wanted to send it to his brother as a gift, with his father. He would buy Khush another camera later. Khush refused. Darshan rang the police, reporting the camera as missing. He gave the police Khushwant's description as a probable suspect.

I was simply unable to take any more. It was time I made my exit, whatever the consequences. To invoke any reason or compassion was impossible. Reluctantly I had to explain to Arune about my decision. On 19 October 1982, Khush and I gave Arune a little birthday party.

On the 20 th, under cover of darkness, while my husband was out, we moved out with the barest essentials.

17

Netherfield—A New Beginning

Life's adversities teach one to look for the positive elements in every situation. What may seem like a calamity, a catastrophe at the time, looks like a mere scratch on the surface later.

I felt very angry and bitter at having to leave my house. I had very little money. Somehow I would have to get together some bare essentials. I had carried on my evening teaching. I note here, with grateful thanks, the help that I received from the parents of pupils I taught. Lynne Hart and her father loaned and connected their spare cooker for me. We managed with some old saris for curtains. Mr and Mrs Hamer gave me an old settee and made sure that the boys got to the Music Centre every Saturday morning. From October to December was a very busy time for musicians. The deputy head at the Centre would not have tolerated slack attendance from her pupils. Dr and Mrs Jones helped with transport and kept in touch constantly to make sure that I wasn't letting the depression of the moment get the better of me.

But the one whose continual support sustained me countless times was my friend, dear Meena Patel. Brought up in a very aristocratic household in India, and having never done any physical labour, she came forward to lend a hand in every way. On the night of my move, she came to help load the small van that I had hired. In doing so she risked Narinder's disapproval. Narinder, Meena's boyfriend, did not want her to associate with me for fear of my 'bad influence'. In his eyes, I was being cruel and heartless to a sick and disabled man.

There were no offers of help from 'family friends'. Most of them were Sikh families and they had condemned my actions. In the past, the children of these friends had spent whole days at my house during the school holidays. They had accompanied me to shows and visits to

London. Yet, at a time of need, they kept away. Not one of these 'family friends' offered to take Khush and Arune away for a day to help cheer up their painfully miserable situation. Perhaps, in times of crisis, one's pride is the only point of strength, keeping one from going right under. My pride had prevented me from asking for any help.

Darshan's nephew, Tarsem, the only person I dared to ask who could have returned some of my favours in kind, said, 'I am sorry Auntyji, I am rather busy at the moment, what with the baby and my car and the house . . . You do understand, don't you? But do ask for help, if you need any.' Of course, I understood. Understanding and compassion had always been one of my stronger points. Perhaps one day I'd forgive him. At the time I felt considerable bitterness and anger. While his uncle had not lifted a finger, I had clocked up hundreds of hours travelling to and fro, making Tarsem's move to Milton Keynes smooth and inexpensive.

The boys and I were determined to succeed. There were only two directions in which this situation could lead us. Either we would disappear into the unfathomable abyss of depression, or we would conquer our obstacles and come out on top, better and stronger for the experience. We decided on the second course. The time had come to explain to Arune about our new situation. He was angry, mostly at having to sleep and play in a room without a carpet and not being allowed to go outside as there was no garden to play in. He missed his father very much, especially the long shopping trips in his daddy's Volvo. He had started answering back and reacting aggressively to most reprimands. Every night he coughed with asthma and came into my bed as usual. As he lay on my stomach and I gently scratched his back, he would say sorry for his temper tantrums. I knew he meant it and could not help his behaviour during the day.

I couldn't say how much of my very simplified explanation Arune understood, but he seemed to calm down a little after that. The next few months showed me the tremendous resilience young children possess. One of Arune's nicest habits is his getting-up routine. Though at times I had found it irritating in the past, at Netherfield it was a blessing. He would get up at the crack of dawn, around six o'clock, dress, clean his teeth and then with his wake-up call, standing there, smiling 'Time to get up Mummy!', he would brighten up the dark, dismal, melancholy mornings. I am sure, if it hadn't been for him, I'd never have made the effort some days.

Despite Meena's constant loving concern, despite Khushwant's strength around me, I felt very depressed. Yes, more than once, I too reproached myself. What was an honourable respectable Indian woman doing in that situation anyway? No wonder I was an object of scorn for my family and friends. How I wished for a letter from my mother though she did not even send Arune a birthday card. I telephoned her to explain, but she did not want to listen. She wrote 'You have dishonoured our *izzat* a second time. Your father and I are old and grey now. You should have thought of that. Your father's condition is poor. High blood pressure has left him very frail. He wants you to come and settle here. He knows a couple of widowers. One of them is a headmaster. We will make your sons into army officers. The West has turned your head. Don't be foolish. Come home.' And the letter went on, 'It is your absolute duty to look after your sick husband. He can't help being violent. The sickness has done this to him. You must take the beatings and help him.'

I did not know whether to laugh or cry. Is this what the system did to women in the end, that she actually believed that my feelings, my children's unhappiness, my very existence indeed, had no meaning unless I carried on bearing physical and verbal abuse from a man of whom the very sight now appalled me? And what about my boys? Khushwant, whose ears must have been sick from hearing the word 'bastard' and the constant bickering in rude Punjabi he only half understood (thank God!). What about his approaching GCE examinations in six months' time? His future education was in the balance. No! My mother had not answered my letter, she had merely stated my father's opinion. Well, opinions did not matter, then. I had to get on with practical decisions. I would seek no more solace. Such expectations only brought hurt and pain.

It was a very painful realisation that my mother could not find it in her heart to share some of my suffering to help me through my darkest hour. For the second time, I was trying hard to build a future from complete ruins. She could have found a little charity for me. I had been thrown into exile and forgotten. Somewhere along the line, my *veer* (brother) had forgotten his *didi* (big sister). Their silence, their rejection of me had culminated in a kind of madness inside my brain.

Why? Why could they not have thrown some crumbs of affection in my direction? Did they not miss me? Ever? A distance of sixteen years and five thousand miles had crushed all relationships into nothingness.

'One main advantage of an arranged marriage is that, in times of crisis, a woman can confidently seek the support of her parents.' A social worker's dogma rang in my ears. Support? Make no mistake, this support is granted on their terms only. Inder-Jeet, my sister, wrote. 'When Daddy is drunk, he cries for you and the boys and says "I want to make it up to Jeet. I want to build a house for her and the boys." When he is sober, he forbids any one to mention your name even.'

Unless I was to agree to a reunion and unconditional reconciliation, they had nothing more to say. Though I felt vulnerable and uncomfortable, I am glad that I was on my own while going through my divorce. Withdrawal of their support made me even more determined to follow my own convictions. Perhaps if my parents had lived near me I would have given in to their emotional pressure, as I later saw many women do. Many of them had been in and out of women's hostels up to six times before finally making up their mind. True, all possibilities of reconciliation should be explored depending upon the circumstances. However, in many instances I have seen women become psychotic cases, unable to cope, unable to make balanced decisions, relying totally on their kinfolk, convinced beyond belief that they know best. Time goes by, and the situation becomes complicated beyond any possibility of rescue or retrieval, particularly in cases when the elders take the children away by force, illegally of course. Where does this tearing apart of a mother-child bond lead to? Yes, there was definitely a positive side to being left alone. I can't begin to imagine the trauma if anyone had tried to take Arune away from me.

Living alone with only a few Asian families around had its advantages too. The only place where the Milton Keynes Sikh community could have openly shown their disapproval would have been at the Neath Hill Gurudwara or any festive functions. I simply kept away from these, and escaped being ostracized and shamed publicly. The gossip would die down in due course, no doubt.

The problems that would face me as a single parent had already begun. At the Netherfield house there was no telephone. I remember how one Sunday in November Arune had a most vicious asthma attack. I gave him the maximum dose of all his medicines, and filled the room with menthol vapours. It was snowing and the wind was very high. Arune was constantly flopping, passing out from lack of breath. The telephone box was some half a mile away. I left Arune to go and make the phone call. I rang Meena. She was not at home. I rang for a taxi. There wasn't one available for the next hour or so. When I got through to the duty doctor, he refused to come out as Netherfield was not in his catchment area. He would see Arune if I were to take him to the surgery, where the doctor was about to hold an emergency session. Eventually I got hold of a taxi, Arune was given an injection and I watched him all night, myself burning with fever as I had caught a chill. Each time something like that happened, I felt myself getting stronger, abandoning passivity and becoming ready to take on my role as a single parent with care, courage and single-mindedness.

I had to make certain that the Parkside house was kept clean, and in saleable condition, so every third day I cycled to the house in the afternoon. Though Darshan was not living there any more, he and his brother kept going back. They would cook dal and leave it to burn to cinders. There would be bits of food, dried up tea bags, empty soup tins and assorted rubbish dumped straight on to the floor. I made a request through the solicitor that if Darshan did not stop making such an abominable mess the property would soon be derelict. Could he please cooperate as he had agreed to abide by the legal document? Next time I went a window had been broken, and I received another of his loathsome letters about women.

The mess was so bad that I had to take the vacuum cleaner with me every time. The window had to be repaired and the shattered glass vacuumed up carefully. One evening I remember, the weather had been miserable. There was an awful slow drizzle of sleet in the air. I was cycling back from Parkside with the vacuum cleaner tied on to the back rack. The bumping must have made it loose. As I rode down the hill to go under the subway the cleaner and the bike went flying in one direction and I landed with a thud, plonk, in a muddy pool of water. Not realising how or what had happened, I threw everything else into the air and just sat there. An elderly lady must have been taking a walk with her dog, for she seemed to appear from nowhere. She helped me to get up and shake some of the mud off.

'Will you be all right child?' She made me laugh. Well! of course I was all right. What else could have possibly happened! I sat in cold muddy pools every day! Arune thought it was funny. 'I didn't know you liked walking through puddles, Mummy!' He always knew how to take the edge off my tension. 'You must admit, Mother dear, you look quite a sight!' said Khush, as he prepared a lovely warm bath for me. I suppose it was more the embarrassment, rather than the physical hurt, that had made me cry.

In more ways than one, Netherfield was a lucky break. It gave me a breathing space in which to assess the implications of my decision for myself and the boys, though the boys didn't feel much at home. From a very practical point of view, over the three months that we stayed at Netherfield I saved up enough to buy the basics for us. Contracts with a buyer were due to be exchanged, when Mr Ghosh, an Indian friend, came round to see me personally and pleaded that I should sell the house to him. I had been teaching his daughter for about a year. I had helped him to secure admission for one of his children to attend the school where I taught. It would be good to help a friend. He was making a private deal with me which meant a saving of fifteen hundred pounds on estate agent's and solicitor's fees. It sounded a very profitable proposition for both of us. The house was being sold at five thousand pounds less than the market value; I was finding it harder to keep cycling some four miles every other day, leaving the boys to fend for themselves. I accepted his promise, believing that he would not delay matters. My house at Furzton was ready and I had received a letter from the corporation asking me for details of the mortgage arrangements. I did not, for a minute, imagine that, of all the people in the world, this so-called friend, an Indian friend, would betray me and take advantage of my tangled predicament. But his own house had not been sold, and he had not been able to secure a mortgage. Another sale had been lost, this time due completely to my own folly. How long would it take? If I didn't find a way to secure a mortgage, my house at Furzton would be offered to someone else after six months.

I went to the Citizen's Advice Bureau for advice on my legal standing. They could offer no help on the mortgage issue, as no building society would release funds until I had paid all monies owed on the joint mortgage. I went to see my bank manager. Like everyone else he said that he shared my anxiety but his hands were tied. The past record on our account was not credit-worthy. Darshan had never allowed me to open an account in my name until a couple of years ago. The joint account was always overdrawn. Lately he had borrowed large sums on our joint credit cards. I was always left in the sticky situation of having to pay or face the court proceedings for non-payment of debts, whatever they might be. Whatever little I could save was always swallowed by these pending overdrafts and unpaid bills. Though we were legally separated, Darshan kept using the cheque cards, thus incurrıng more debts. I had always wanted to change my name, though not seriously at first; but the devious ways in which he used my name to borrow money, convinced me that once I'd changed my name by deed poll, I would no longer be liable for his misdemeanour. I adopted the name Shan, from the nickname 'Shanno' Aziz had sometimes given me, a word meaning grace, dignity and pride.

All I could do was wait. And then a ray of hope shone through. Suzanne Hopkins, a pupil of mine at Denbigh suggested I talked to her father, a bank manager. My own bank manager had refused me, but I guessed there would be no harm in taking a second opinion. Bless her heart! Suzanne never told me exactly what she said to her dad. Mr Hopkins looked closely at all the documents, including my meagre efforts at savings over the past six months. Within a week he wrote to formally confirm that if I had not been successful in effecting a completion or exchange of contracts on the sale of the Parkside house, he would be prepared to advance me the required sum to purchase a share in the plot in Furzton. He also advised that I should not give more than two months to Mr Ghosh to come up with an exchange of contracts. It would be in my interest to put the house back on the market. At its very low price, there would be plenty of buyers.

By the beginning of January 1983, Mr Ghosh's own house was sold and provisional papers were signed. The mortgage was released later in January and I got the keys for the new house. Arune was so excited. It was the realisation of my determination to provide a little home for us where we could live with self-respect and dignity.

For Khush, it was a tremendous relief. He had helped his mother to seek out a solution for a major problem. I felt so proud of him. He still had four months left in which to prepare for his exams. He had been working hard already; now he would be able to do it in a calmer frame of mind.

The three of us were exhausted but at peace, at last.

18

How I Put the Ghost to Rest

Decree Absolute was granted in March 1983. 'Free to make my own choices and independent decisions. Free to learn from my own mistakes.' This privilege was at last mine.

All the while that the divorce proceedings were going through, there was an undercurrent of fear that the time had to come to take a decision regarding Aziz. Every day, in my moments of solitude, I had argued and struggled with the loud and clear call to rationalise my feelings and act intelligently. In his last few telephone calls and letters Aziz had talked only of his wife and how he had succeeded at last in restoring peace with her. The decreasing frequency of his telephone calls was explained by his concern for his wife. The transient happenings during my divorce had tried my tenacity in every way. I had stopped calling him. It was best to put it out of my mind lest I should do something foolish.

One thing I had come to understand for certain. There would never be any further physical manifestation of my love for him. What an irony, to have touched him so closely, to have reached my destination, my Mecca, my Medina, and then to force myself to walk away. For his sake? Maybe. For my own sake then? Who knows? 'If you truly love a man, no personal sacrifice is considered enough for the sake of his happiness.' The equation had been a very straightforward one in my book. My prayers had been answered; my search had come to an end. A hard fact though it was to swallow, the time had come to put my philosophy into practice. To cause him even a slight suffering on my behalf was unthinkable. And yet I did not know how I would reconcile myself to a life of just waiting for him, without expecting my love to be reciprocated.

Every time the phone rang, I'd jump, I'd be in an uncontrollable state of emotional turmoil. I used to think I'd go insane. The most wonderful city in the world seemed to have every wretched phone box vandalised. Sometimes it took him a whole hour to find a phone box and while waiting I'd walk about like a zombie. Stealing himself away for a few minutes one day while the family did the shopping, he rang from a department store. I picked up the phone. His money would not go in, and he had to go to another floor to find a phone box that worked. I had not heard from him for over three weeks. When he did get through, he sounded so tired and depressed. 'Shanno! I don't want to cause any unhappiness to my wife and children.' Then after a long pause, 'It's not as if you are miserable down there and I am enjoying life. I miss you dreadfully, but tell me what to do . . . You'd have to be strong for the both of us. *Tumken sabar karna hoga.*' 'You would have to be patient.' And then he ended his barely audible, hurried conversation with 'Remember, I love you—always. Only a man has to do his duty. Doesn't he?'

Time and again, I thought of his wife. She had not done me any harm. I felt quite disgusted that I had upset their peaceful and pleasant life together. I did not wish to go on haunting him like a dark shadow. After all, I had sought him out. I was guilty of introducing conflict into his life. And yet I had wanted to cry out in defence of my mortal soul, trapped in a living body, for the feelings that had been unlocked and needed expression now. I could not bear the thought of losing him a second time. Was I capable of continuing a platonic relationship? Not asking to see him, ever? The time had come perhaps, to test it out.

Oh yes, *sabar*—patience, that was quite something else, described in Urdu poetry as an immensely enchanting and boundless virtue, especially possessed by true lovers. It all sounded so shallow and pretentious. *Kismet*, fate, was laughing at me, challenging me yet again to see if I had any strength left. 'An act of supreme sacrifice elevates a human to the position of a *farishta*—an angel of the highest order,' says a *shabad* from the Adi Granth. Had I not made my share of sacrifices? Had I not paid for my guilt? Physically and emotionally, I felt exhausted, burnt out. For a second time I had tried to put together the fragments of broken hopes. Had I exchanged one dream for another, or had I touched reality?

During mid-February Aziz phoned to say that there would be a possibility of his visiting me in April. Khush and I got busy with various chores that needed attending to in a new house. We wanted to get the house ready for his visit. I was so looking forward to the boys meeting Aziz. But it was not to be. His family changed their plans at the last minute, but he would be able to stop for a few minutes on his way to London. It was then, as he stood in my kitchen drinking coffee, that I realised the overwhelming tension and uneasiness in him. I suppose that he must have realised that he was betraying his wife. I myself felt very uncomfortable and confused. A mixture of fatigue and a feeling of defeat, perhaps?

'You're very quiet,' he said. What could I have said? That I had suddenly become conscious of my one-sided monologue with my dream? That I did not feel free at all, that I was feeling like a fish out of water? This man, I had just introduced to my children as a 'special friend', was not my Aziz. This was definitely a stranger. Our paths were separate, our worlds were apart.

Lost in his embrace for those few last minutes, I felt very empty. He praised the boys and said that I had done remarkably well and that I had been very lucky. I tried to conceal my irritation. What did luck have to do with it? It had been an uphill climb all the way. Leaving him at the motorway, I returned home feeling numb and depleted of all energy. The reality, that life with Aziz was unattainable, was staring me in the face. It was time to accept the hopelessness of our relationship. Within minutes I had worked myself up into a frenzy. I don't think my boys had ever seen me in such a totally uncontrollable fit of tears and sobs. Khush was furious. 'Big deal, Mother!' he shouted at the top of his voice. 'To be with him, twice a year, and on what terms? Are you mad or something?' There were tears lurking in those big brown eyes. He sat me down by sheer brute force, made me a cup of tea and said that, though he held me in very high esteem, he was simply fed up of what I was doing to myself. Why was I prepared to waste my energies in this way? He could not understand what was making me go through any amount of inconvenience to seek such an unreal arrangement. 'It just wouldn't work and what's more, you know it.'

As he tucked me up in bed, I knew that the time had come to end this suffering. Dreams may be shadows of reality for some. This was not even a glimpse of a shadow for me. Was I now going to waste precious life grieving over what was not to be? Everything else had been put right, fallen into place. All my life, I had loved this one man. That love had been my faith and my hope. Only now, there were more important issues at stake. There were his children, his wife and his deep involvement in his work. And wasn't my son voicing a truly rational, balanced point of view? I did deserve better than to let a dream go on punishing me. All night long, I did a lot of soul searching. Eternal love was simply a mirage of the mind. I was chasing illusions. Only my young son's viewpoint reflected reality.

My birds were gradually awakening from their night-long sleep. In the early hours of the morning, I wrote a very brief letter to Aziz. 'The time has come to cut my cord with the past. The twenty-year-old ghost living inside me must die, so that I may live, so that a measure of calm may descend on my life. Please believe me, I do understand your commitment to your family. Look after your wife and yourself. Allah be with you, and keep you safe—always.'

So there it was, the twenty-year-old ghost of my youth, that had been looming large over the horizon threatening to destroy my life yet again, had been killed at last. I would not have to go on in a meaningless limbo. In searching out my reality and facing it, the lessons I learnt were perhaps the most rewarding of all. The capacity of the human mind for endurance of suffering in love is both fascinating and intriguing. After listening to such a lot of courageous women, both Indian and British, and hearing how so many live out the best years of their life compromising within this most important woman-man relationship, the healing process for my own torn spirit had begun. I had been very fortunate in being given a second chance.

By September 1983 life was gradually starting to settle down. Arune-Preet had formed a very warm relationship, all on his own, with his teacher, Julie Farid. Julie had been married very happily to an Arab Muslim until his unfortunate death due to cancer. She had more than an average understanding of Asian people and had sympathised with Arune and me ever since we first met. With her help and loving care, Arune was learning to cope with the inevitable tensions and confusions within himself. His whimpering and moaning was disappearing.

I am sure his lack of cooperation was due to his inability to understand and cope with my miserable frame of mind. All his childhood he knew a mum who was fun to be with, who could be relied upon always. The last two years had been a living hell. I suppose under normal circumstances it would have been common sense to see that my disquiet and agitation were bound to affect them in some way. I should have recognised some of this anxiety when I had heard Khush say to Arune countless times, 'Leave Mummy alone. Can't you see she is upset?' My permanent panic-stricken state must have baffled Arune. His school work had suffered badly. He had become diffident and quarrelsome. By nature, he was an extrovert, but not cantankerous. I was much too busy with solicitors, court appearances and estate agents, trying to establish a roof over our heads, to realise the psychological and emotional ill-effects of the instability of the situation on my little one. I had had to ignore him constantly. It was all over now though. He was adjusting to his new way of life very well. I was trying to make it up to him. There were only the financial limitations of a single parent; otherwise, nothing much had changed for him. With his brilliantly inquisitive mind, he had always had plenty to search for, look at and enjoy. It was a joy to hear him singing around the house again.

Khushwant too did well with his 'O' level examinations and his violin. He and his friend won the award for the best performance at the Milton Keynes Festival of Arts 1983. Khushwant also secured for himself an apprenticeship with a very reputable firm in electronic engineering. He understood that we were not a conventional family and he took on the responsibility towards his younger brother with great sensitivity and cheerfulness. Of course, they often fought, as brothers do, but there was a unique closeness born out of the frowns of fortune. There was an unwritten agreement between us not to let each other down, ever.

My parents had stopped writing to me altogether. Their rejection of me for a second time was a hurt that cut too deep to express in words. I did understand their extreme revulsion for my actions. There was no forgiveness for the humiliation I had brought upon them.

Did I regard the Indian community and my relatives with contempt? Far from it. Though I never intended adopting the patronising and condescending ways of either the English or the Indian community, I had now accepted that I was an object of ridicule through my own actions, as I had dared to rebel against the time-honoured system. I did not bear any grudges or grievances against my ex-husband any more. He was brought up to demand total subjugation and slavishness from a wife. His resentment of my independent spirit may not have been fair, but was understandable. Who knows, he might have made a successful marriage with someone more submissive than me.

Though Darshan had been denied legal access, I had agreed to allow him to see Arune once in a while, so long as he complied with the simple condition of behaving in a gentle, agreeable manner. This was purely for Arune's sake; I would not have wished to deny him access to his father. Darshan had declared himself a saint. There were very impressive advertisements in the city papers; how he was going to build a hostel for destitute men and women (I suppose he was expecting me to be his first customer!). People were being asked to become members of this glorious organisation for the benefit of their souls. He claimed to have secured funds towards the building. Simultaneously he had set himself up as a businessman, hiring out video equipment and films. He had, apparently, adopted the lifestyle he had always wanted, a lifestyle to which I had been a hindrance.

Then I started to receive quite disgusting letters from Darshan at school. These included quotations from famous black women writers about their slavery, and Asian women working as nannies. There was a letter demanding ten thousand pounds for the jewellery that he was supposed to have given me. One such letter came by recorded delivery from his solicitor, ordering me to pay a large sum of money or appear in court. There was a long explanation of how I had defaulted on the agreement made in court by leaving Mr Jabble to fend for himself between October and January 1983. The letter also stated that this was a compensatory allowance being claimed from me as I had left the matrimonial home of my own accord. In the same letter, he requested me to encourage the children to visit him, though understanding their disinclination.

I ignored the letter, and decided to see if he would pursue the case through court. It would have been quite easy to prove that Darshan had not kept his side of the agreement. By not signing the contract, by starting fires in the kitchen and living room, by not paying the mortgage, he had not exactly done his best to 'ensure a speedy completion'.

He turned up at Arune-Preet's school threatening to take him away and to 'do away with me' with a gun. 'She does not deserve to live', he argued with the headmistress. The school coordinated admirably with mine to remove Arune from the scene. When I was made aware of this incident I had no choice but to contact my solicitor. If Darshan was going to continue his harassment tactics, he must not be allowed to see the boys again. We were divorced. He had no right to threaten me. By June 1983, over a period of some eight months, he had written some thirty-five letters, each one a threat, stating how some day he would take his revenge upon me.

Sometimes, when Darshan passed me in the city centre, it was hard to believe that we were now total strangers, I and this man whom fate and an arranged marriage had made my husband. I had no feelings for him of any kind any more.

The mood of his letters suddenly changed in July. There were now requests to see the boys. He was feeling very lonely and wanted to see Arune at any cost even if Khush didn't want to see him. I phoned the Churchill Hospital and had it confirmed that Darshan's health was deteriorating fast. He was refusing to cooperate with the doctors, nurses and even the ambulance men. Arune kept refusing to go. He must have wanted to see his father very much, but had such conflicting memories to sort out. Together Julie Farid and I managed to persuade him. Their first meeting went smoothly, and we arranged that they meet regularly from then on.

But in October 1983 Darshan died.

That afternoon, Julie accompanied me to see Darshan's solicitor so that I could secure the release of the body for cremation. All he had to do was to telephone the hospital administrator to vouch for me and let me have the death certificate, but for some reason, the solicitor blinded me with the most incomprehensible legal jargon. I did not wish to get involved in the winding up of my husband's estate. All I wanted was to cremate my husband with full Sikh tradition and dignity. Every human being deserves a decent burial or cremation. I came back home in utter confusion, unable to swallow the inopportune expediency of the solicitor.

All I could think of was that, if I did not get on with cremation arrangements, the hospital would want to dispose of the body. The whole thing was so painful to Arune. He kept asking me questions I could not answer. He kept hiding in corners and crying. If I tried to comfort him he screamed back at me that I had killed Daddy and that we should never have left him. I had to do something for my son's sake. A proper cremation with full traditional service was absolutely essential. Surely, there was someone who could advise me better!

Then I thought of Colin Hopkins, my bank manager, who had proffered such practical advice in the past. At first he thought it inadvisable to spend more than half my savings on the cremation of my ex-husband, but after some discussion he appreciated my sentiments and the importance of a proper service on behalf of the children. He telephoned the Northampton Trust where wills are registered. Naturally, Khush was the next of kin. As he was only sixteen years old, I had to act on his behalf. In the eyes of the law, an ex-wife has no connection. The various authorities concerned were finally convinced that by cremating my husband I would not benefit in any way. Colin telephoned the hospital administrator, who was very agreeable from then on, then later that afternoon he and his wife accompanied me to Oxford to register the death. Early that morning, I had felt so helpless and distraught. I could never put it in words, the gratitude I felt to those two lovely people. Darshan's relatives rang to say that I was being very selfish and that I should make arrangements to fly the body home to Darshan's parents in India.

Mr Matthews, the funeral director, came to see me at home to discuss the arrangements. I was greatly impressed by his awareness and sensitivity not only to our grief, but also to the traditional Sikh way of cremation. There were no more than forty or fifty Sikh families in the city of Milton Keynes, and yet this gentle Englishman had taken the trouble to acquaint himself with our ways. When there were such people around, how could anyone ever scorn me for being 'eternally optimistic'?

I contacted Mr Singh, the president of the Milton Keynes Gurudwara Committee. Together with a renowned priest he took charge of the arrangements for the ceremony. I was given complete guidance on the preparation, so that nothing should go wrong. For a Sikh it is considered most important to do *Allahnia Ji da Path*, the very special prayer from the Adi Granth, after the cremation of the body. This is to facilitate the liberation of the soul and pray for it to enter the realm of grace (*sach khand*). In the Sikh faith there is no belief in reincarnation as a human being or life after death. The future of the soul is decid-

171

ed on the basis of its actions while in the world. It may be reborn as an animal if its development is not complete. It is to avoid this wandering that *Allahnia Ji da Path* was devised.

If one can ever think of a funeral being a nice event, I would note here that it was indeed a very 'nice' funeral, a quiet, dignified affair. Part of the service was conducted at my house. Darshan's brother and sister-in-law arrived just half an hour before the cremation. There was very little for me to say to them. All my married life, I had kept my peace, always observing proper etiquette. It would have been very regrettable to have made a fool of myself then.

Mr Singh performed the ceremony of wrapping the body in a new cloth. (This is normally carried out by a brother.) Traditionally the oldest son should ignite the fire; Arune wanted to perform this last rite alongside his big brother, Khush, but it was considered inadvisable by the other adults present. I was to regret this later, as for months Arune struggled to understand the meaning of cremation. In a few moments it was all over. It is forbidden in Britain to throw the ashes into a river. This would be the proper course of action in India. I could have requested the Anglia Water Authority to let me do this somewhere in running water, but the idea of burying the ashes in the Garden of Rest appealed to me more. Besides, I wanted a rose bush planted in Darshan's name. It made more sense to have his ashes in the same place.

I said a quiet prayer.

As a million sparks rise from a single fire,
Separate and come together as they fall back into it.
As from a heap of dust, grains are blown upwards,
Fill the air and then drop back on to the heap.
As drops of water come from a single stream and return to it,
So inanimate and live creation emerged from God's form
And since they arise from him, they will return again.'

(*Akal Ustat*—a translation by W Owen Cole and Piara Singh Sambhi)

Where do I go from here? Though the loneliness of the future casts a gloom sometimes, I certainly do not want any more dreams. Has the trauma of the horrific memories of the past etched a deep scar on my psyche? Who knows? A feeling of awkwardness fills me. For me there is no room for self-pity and tears. I have to learn to conquer my inhibitions, bred into me by tradition. The present seems relaxed and calm.

Sometimes I wonder if, like my sons, I too have a conflict. Am I a proper Indian? If I was to preserve the true image of an educated and enlightened Indian parent, I would be pushing my sons to go to university at any cost. I could only be classed as a true Sikh if I went to the Gurudwara every Sunday, grew my hair long and never wore a dress. I would not discuss any issues affecting my children's future, simply make loud pronouncements, expecting them to follow unquestioningly. I would be investigating young girls as prospective mates for my sons.

Both Darshan's relatives and my own have approached me with a view to arranging a marriage for Khush who, in their eyes, is an 'attractive catch'. 'Over my dead body,' is my concise answer to that. Hopefully my son will make his own relationship when he is ready. He understands that one does not walk into a life-long alliance blindly. The most important association of one's life is not arranged or made in heaven. It has to be worked at with body and mind. Of course, there will be ups and downs on the way. Isn't that what life is all about?

As I have failed miserably in the practice of the prudent, philanthropic characteristics of a true Indian, I suppose I am, as a colleague of mine calls me jokingly (I hope) 'an Indian reject'. This label was bestowed on me at the dinner table one lunch hour when, instead of jumping with joy at the school's curry cuisine, I had opted for a ploughman's. As a Sikh woman, I do not observe or keep the symbols of the faith. As a divorced woman, I cannot lay claim to any prestige standing in the community. So what am I? Who am I now? Well, perhaps I shall have a distinctive identity of my very own.

As for my two sons, I feel convinced that despite their experiences, or maybe because of them, they are well prepared to promote good relations, an *entente cordiale* between Britain and India. A unique appreciation of the variety of both cultures is reflected in their lifestyle. I can only hope and pray that an authentic identity will be born out of this assemblage of the East and the West. Does it sound eccentric, over-optimistic? Perhaps so. But the truth of the matter is, children like mine have no religion, no strong family ties to fall back on in times of crisis. As a parent I can only ensure that my sons should experience a strong feeling of love and belonging, and of trust, that most precious gift of all.

I am not so critical of the self-indulgent ways of the West any more, though a lot of them remain basically alien to me. I am, however, beginning to taste the joy of freedom, the joy of making a choice without fear of ridicule and reprehension, the joy of cooking my children's favourite dishes, the joy of listening to my favourite pieces of music and reading my favourite newspaper lying in bed on a Sunday morning. I want to live a little for me now.

In my search for a reality of my own, I have realised that I find a tremendous satisfaction in promoting the cause of multi-culturalism, be it in the art form or via the educational system. I have started to carve out a new career for myself in the Youth and Community Service. I would like to employ my newly-learnt skills in some service for women and girls in India some day. The hope of living and working in India, my country, my home, gets stronger in my heart every day. Meanwhile, I must study to improve my qualifications. From the bewildered, naïve twenty-year-old who stepped off the plane full of apprehensive hostility, who looked at the dark grey English sky, I have come a long way. Of course, the unknown, unpredictable future will bring its own surprises. I am ready for those.

As you read

Before you begin
In pairs, look at the front cover and the title.
- What clues are you given to this book?
- What might be the meaning of the title?

Now read the description of the book on the back cover. Does this support your interpretation?

A reading log
Keep a reading log which records your impressions of *In My Own Name* as you read. View your reading log as a kind of diary where you can note down feelings and thoughts as they occur to you. It should provide plenty of ideas for coursework assignments later on.

In your reading log, aim to:

Record key events, perhaps critical moments in Sharan-Jeet's life, which make an impression on you.

Ask questions about aspects of plot, character, setting, themes and the style of writing which you find puzzling or intriguing.

Reminisce about experiences and memories of your own, sparked off by your reading.

Compare this autobiography with books you have read with a similar subject, or with other autobiographies.

Predict what is going to happen at key moments in the narrative and say why you think this.

Reflect upon some of the ideas, themes, thoughts and feelings expressed and give your reactions to them.

Comment on any aspects of the book's style – that is, the variety of ways in which language is used to tell the story.

Assess how much you are enjoying the autobiography; what you find interesting about it; and whether you would recommend it to other readers, giving your reasons why.

A glossary

Make a note of all the Hindu/Urdu words which are used in
this book, in order to compile a glossary of important terms.
Perhaps focus on single words which recur, like *izzat* (family
honour), rather than upon whole phrases. When you have
finished reading, design a glossary listing the words in
alphabetical order, and explaining their meanings. This may
help you with future pieces of coursework.

The range of activities which follow take you through the
text and help you to focus on themes, issues, and features
of autobiographical writing. Do not expect to do **all** the
activities here – select the ones which interest you, and suit
your method of study. The work you do in this section will
help you to prepare for the coursework assignments in
After Reading on pp. 183–188.

From p. 177 onwards, the activities are grouped under
chapter headings. Look briefly at these activities before you
read each chapter.

Chapters 1 – 3

Predicting Sharan-Jeet Shan's life

At the end of chapter 1, the writer looks back at her life and asks a number of questions about the sad position she finds herself in.

Using any clues given in the first chapter, discuss in pairs what you imagine the answers to her questions might be. Have you revised any of the predictions you made in 'Before you begin' (p. 175)?

Understanding

In chapters 2 and 3, Sharan-Jeet Shan describes her childhood in some detail. She shows that, from the very beginning of her life, she was 'born to be *parai*' (someone else's property).

In groups, find evidence which shows the difference in her parents' attitude towards their son and daughter. Make your notes in two columns like this:

Sharan-Jeet	Param-Jeet
1. Expected to share everything with her brother.	1. Gets far more attention from his parents than his sister does.

Now turn your notes into a series of statements. For example, 'Sharan-Jeet was expected to share everything with her brother.'

In your groups, discuss how true each statement is to your own lives. Do parents tend to treat brothers and sisters differently?

Chapters 4 – 6

Understanding

In chapter 4, Sharan-Jeet explains a number of concepts which she says are an important part of the Indian way of life. From your reading of this chapter and your own experience, discuss in groups what you understand by each concept below.

- *izzat* (family honour)
- *purdah* (concealment)
- *pativarta istry* (one who worships her husband as God)
- the caste system
- arranged marriages and the dowry system
- reincarnation (*karma*, *dharma* and *nirvana*)

Give your own opinion of each concept, as far as you understand it. Say to what extent your opinion matches, or differs from, Sharan-Jeet's.

Role-playing

Read as far as chapter 6. In pairs, discuss which issues tend to cause most disagreement between parents and teenage children. Are parents justified in getting angry with you, or are they generally being unreasonable?

Together, work out a scene between a parent and a teenager where there is a reason for strong disagreement. Try acting the scene with one of you as the parent, the other as the teenager; then, swap over your roles, choose another issue and play the scene again. What did each of you learn about the parent's point of view?

Chapters 7 – 9

Understanding

Sharan-Jeet describes how problems emerge in her marriage, from the moment she arrives in England. Use these three chapters to analyse the reasons for 'the growing rift' between Sharan-Jeet and Darshan. In pairs, note the evidence you find under the headings below (or similar ones of your own):

1 Hardships in England
2 Personal incompatibilities
3 Other causes.

Share your ideas with another pair and discuss who or what is mainly responsible for the 'growing rift' between the couple.

Role-playing

During chapters 7–9, Sharan-Jeet describes various sources of conflict between herself and Darshan. In pairs or groups, develop a role-play based on one of the following quotations from these chapters:

My brother-in-law, Hardev, lived on social security and us. All the time that he stayed with us, it was free board and lodging. p. 59

I tried hard to get him to work out a routine which would make it possible to share the household chores. p. 63 and also see p. 73

I was very doubtful of my physical strength in taking on this task [of turfing the lawn] single-handed, but knew that Darshan and I could easily do it together. p. 72 and also see p. 73

The bare fact was that [Darshan] had fallen deeply into debt, whilst keeping his parents in a constant state of delusion as to his wealth. p. 74 and also see pp. 75–76

Decide who is to be involved in the role-play. For example, you may wish to include a third person such as Hardev, Khushwant, Mr Childs or Penny Jones. Use the narrative as the source of ideas for the role-play, either to act out a scene which is actually described or to create a scene which *might* have happened.

Chapters 10 – 12

Letter to a problem page
Yet I felt I needed help.   p. 106

At the end of chapter 11, Sharan-Jeet describes a critical moment in her marriage to Darshan. Despite her reluctance to consult outside agencies, imagine that she decides to send a letter to the 'agony aunt' of a well-known woman's magazine. She asks the 'agony aunt' not to publish her letter but to send her a private reply. Reread chapter 11 carefully; then draft the letter she might have written at this point in her life, describing her problems and asking for advice.

When you have written your letter, work with a partner who has also done this exercise. In the role of 'agony aunt', draft a reply to your *partner's* letter.

An alternative point of view
Poor Mother though! I am sure she was thoroughly perplexed by the whole episode.   p. 116

Write an alternative version of chapter 12, as if you are Sharan-Jeet's mother visiting England for the very first time. Imagine how high your expectations might be about England, 'the land of milk and honey'. Also imagine your hopes for your daughter's marriage to Darshan, as well as your excitement about seeing your grandsons.

To prepare for this work, reread chapter 12 in order to understand Mother's character and viewpoint. Consider how she might react to the real conditions of her daughter's life. Would she feel resigned to fate, or would she feel determined to help her daughter in some way?

Chapters 13 – 15

Discussing statements

These chapters chart the events which led to Sharan-Jeet's separation and, eventually, to her divorce from Darshan. Do you think that she took the right course of action? To answer this, discuss in groups which of the following statements you tend to agree with and which not, giving your reasons:

- *Sharan-Jeet was wrong to have a love affair with Aziz.*
- *Darshan was not to blame for the breakdown of the marriage – he was a very sick man.*
- *Adultery was not the reason for the marriage breakdown. Sharan-Jeet should have divorced her husband on grounds of unreasonable behaviour.*
- *Sharan-Jeet and Darshan should have stayed together for the sake of their two sons.*
- *Sharan-Jeet was right to take her destiny into her own hands and seek an independent life.*

A solicitor's brief

In pairs, imagine you are both solicitors acting on behalf of clients who wish to get a divorce. One of you will act for Sharan-Jeet and the other for Darshan. Although you are both more likely to be sympathetic towards Sharan-Jeet than Darshan, try to see the defence of Darshan as a challenge – after all, the reasons for the marriage break-down are not straightforward.

As the solicitor, your brief is to gather evidence which defends your client. Suppose that the divorce charge were to be changed from 'adultery' to 'unreasonable behaviour'. To do this, find evidence from the text which appears to defend the actions of your client, and to condemn the actions of 'the other party'.

Then present your client's case to other members of the class. Ask them to judge which 'solicitor' has presented the more convincing case.

Chapters 16 – 18

A post-mortem

Despite the terrible ordeal of the divorce, the autobiography appears to end on a positive note. In groups, discuss the outcome of the book by role-playing one of these people who influenced Sharan-Jeet's life:

- Mother
- Babuji
- Darshan
- Papaji (Darshan's father)
- Aziz
- Khushwant.

Before your discussion begins, prepare a few notes on the person you will play. The aim of the activity is to give your view of how Sharan-Jeet's life has turned out, and to discuss your own part in her 'destiny'. This is the chance for the person you are role-playing to:

- express regrets
- give explanations
- make apologies
- express feelings
- justify your behaviour
- question other people about their behaviour
- say what you have learnt
- say whether you will behave differently in the future.

Try to stay in role for the duration of the discussion. Remember that everything you say should be entirely consistent with the text.

Discussion

I believe that everyone should be free to tell a personal story if they choose to.   Author's Introduction

Do you think Sharan-Jeet was right to tell her 'personal story'? Her introduction explains how she felt compelled to speak out about her 'personal oppression'. By writing an *autobiography*, rather than, say, *fiction*, she chose to share her own life, as well as those of her family and friends, with other people.

In groups or as a class, discuss whether 'everyone should be free to tell a personal story if they choose to', or whether, for good reasons, there should be some exceptions.

After reading

The coursework assignments here are based on your reading of the whole novel. They offer suggestions both for individual written work, and for oral performance. Before starting an assignment, please read the author's introduction again – it may provide some useful resource material.

1 A wall frieze
Design a wall chart or frieze which records dates and episodes in Sharan-Jeet's life from birth to mature womanhood. Give your wall chart a particular focus which will determine your choice of graphic design. For example, if you wish to record life-changing decisions, you might draw a flow-chart. If you would rather indicate high and low moments in her life, consider drawing a line graph.

2 Your autobiography
Write a chapter for your own autobiography. Either use a chapter heading similar to one of those used in *In My Own Name*, or think of a specific incident or experience in the past which may have changed your life. For example:

- The Accident
- Moving House
- Leaving My Country
- Starting School
- A Friendship
- The Death of . . .

Try to make your autobiography seem real to the reader, so that she or he can relive and identify with your own experiences. Avoid simply recording what happened to you chronologically. Instead, use the theme of the chapter to organise what you have to say; describe the people and places involved; use dialogue to dramatise episodes and explain how you felt and thought.

3 Biography of someone you know

Write the biography of someone you know who has lived life to the full and is prepared to talk to you about it. She or he might be a relative, a friend of your parents, a parent of one of your friends, a neighbour or a local 'character'. Prepare for this by writing down a number of questions before you talk to them. If possible, tape record the conversation. Then, using your notes and tape-recording, write out their life story. You may need to edit their words to make a lively and readable account.

4 Tape-recorded reading

In groups make a tape-recorded reading of an extract from *In My Own Name* to play back to readers who do not know the book. Choose an extract which might make a dramatic impact upon your audience and which gives a strong indication of the book's themes.

If you like, retell your extract as a radio-play using introductory music, sound effects, dialogue, and short pieces of narrative to link and make sense of each new scene.

5 A conversation in the future

The inspiration for writing my autobiography came from my desire to sort out my confusion about my father.

Author's introduction

Imagine a time in the future when Sharan-Jeet and her father might meet again. Suppose that the passing of time has cooled their emotions to a certain extent. Write the conversation they might have together about difficulties in the past. Sharan-Jeet might put forward her views about arranged marriages, divorce and the need for women to achieve freedom from oppression. Her father might offer his own views with explanations about his past behaviour. Try to give equal weight to each speaker, showing the reasoning behind their differing views. To prepare for this assignment, read the Author's introduction at the beginning of the book.

6 A film of the book

Choose one chapter, or an episode within a chapter, which you feel would work very well on film. Be sure to reread it carefully, considering how you might go about filming it. Then follow these guidelines to help you produce a script for sound and camera:

a. Use a form like the one below to give your instructions about the camera shots, and a description of what is on the sound track at any one time.

b. The sound track is likely to be mainly dialogue with some music and sound effects. Consider whether you will use a narrator as a 'voice over', who explains the links between scenes.

c. Use sketches (line drawings or stick people will do), to show the subject of each visual frame. Number each frame in sequence.

d. To show the camera movements between each visual frame, use the standard coding:

CU	Close-up	(face or detail)
FI	Fade-in	
FO	Fade-out	
LS	Long shot	(group or scene in total)
MCU	Medium close-up	(face and half body)
PAN	Pan	(swing camera around a scene)
ZI/ZO	Zoom in/zoom out	

No.	Visual	Camera Shot	Sound
1			
2			

7 Discussion essays

a. *[My mother] was beginning to understand that struggling alone in my isolated circumstances had changed my personality.* Chapter 12, p. 112

Throughout the sixteen years of her marriage, Sharan-Jeet struggled for an independent existence of her own. Look at the pressures which made her life such a struggle. Show how these pressures changed her personality. Do you feel that all the changes were for the better?

b. *[Darshan] was brought up to demand subjugation and slavishness from a wife. His resentment of my independent spirit may not have been fair, but was understandable.* Chapter 18, p. 169

Make a case in defence of Darshan's behaviour in the book. Referring closely to textual evidence, consider such factors as: his upbringing, his illness, his difficulties living in a foreign land, the demands of his relatives, and his incompatibility with his wife.

c. *Darshan and I were two of the most incompatible personalities, emotionally, physically and mentally. There was no companionship, no friendliness between us.* Chapter 9, p. 73

Does the autobiography imply that Sharan-Jeet and Darshan were equally responsible for the marriage breakdown? By referring closely to the text, show which factors led to their divorce and discuss whether or not we are given a balanced view of what happens.

d. *'Marriage should be based on a complete understanding, a perfect union of minds.'*

President Nehru, Chapter 4, p. 28

Social compatibility was seen as important, but love, as my father had advised me many times, had nothing whatsoever to do with marriage. p. 28

What is your own view of arranged marriages? Drawing on your knowledge of the subject, your reading of *In My Own Name* and possibly your own experience, make a case either for or against them. Say how far you agree or disagree with Sharan-Jeet's view of arranged marriages.

e. How does this autobiography successfully reconstruct the reality of the past? Consider the ways in which Sharan-Jeet enables the reader to enter into her world, to relive and to identify with her feelings and her point of view. You might consider her use of techniques such as:

- narrative
- dramatised action
- varied mood and pace
- description of people and places
- dialogue
- internal monologue – expressing her inner feelings and thoughts
- characterisation

Choose one chapter from the book which you found interesting. Write a detailed study of the methods used to bring the past alive, giving examples from the text.

f. *Why did the happiness of a few moments always have to be paid for with separation and the grief of a thousand?*
Chapter 14, p. 139

This is how Sharan-Jeet describes her doomed relationship with Aziz. To what extent was she a victim of her circumstances? Do you feel that she was really trapped by fate? By close study of the main crisis points in her life, argue either that she was indeed trapped by fate, or that she acted as effectively as she could to alter the course of her life.

g. *I was always an Indian and an immigrant first, a teacher and a human being second.* Chapter 11, p. 104

Is this a fair summary of Sharan-Jeet's experience as an immigrant in Britain? From your reading of her autobiography, decide whether her experience was generally a positive or a negative one. Look closely at the friendships she makes and the hostilities she receives before making your judgement.

8 Further discussion topics

Sharan-Jeet Shan, herself a teacher, has suggested this list of discussion statements, 'in order to complete the picture of how I see young people benefitting from my book'.

In groups, discuss which of these statements you agree with, and which you do not. Try to find evidence to support your views, both from *In My Own Name* and from your own experience.

a. *White women often suppose that they are far more free than Black and Asian women in their choice of careers and in marriage.*

b. *British society is a class-ridden society, not least in education.*

c. *Asian women are wrong to speak out against arranged marriages. This will only provoke racial hostility against Asian people.*

d. *Whether a marriage is arranged or based on love, it is a barrier to freedom.*

e. *Marriage offers security: two people can depend on each other on every level – physical, social, financial and intellectual.*

You may wish to consider one of these statements more fully. This could take the form of:

- carrying out a class/year survey to find out how many people agree or disagree with the statement;
- holding a class debate to discuss the subject more thoroughly;
- writing a discussion essay in which you explore your own views and compare them with the views presented in *In My Own Name*.